m/cs

D1415190

м

DRUMS OF MORNING

Drums
of Morning

Growing Up in the Thirties

Vernon Scannell

SASKATOON PUBLIC LIBRARY

ISIS
LARGE PRINT
Oxford, England

Copyright © 1992 Vernon Scannell

First published in Great Britain 1992
by Robson Books Ltd

Published in Large Print 1995 by ISIS Publishing Ltd,
7 Centremead, Osney Mead, Oxford OX2 0ES,
by arrangement with Robson Books Ltd

All rights reserved

The moral right of the author has been asserted.

British Library Cataloguing in Publication Data
Scannell, Vernon
    Drums of Morning: Growing Up in the
    Thirties. – New ed
    I. Title
    821.914

ISBN 1-85695-122-7

Printed and bound by Hartnolls Ltd, Bodmin, Cornwall

To Kenneth & Jenny Bain

Up, lad, up 'tis late for lying:
  Hear the drums of morning play;
Hark, the empty highways crying
  "Who'll beyond the hills away?"

From *Reveille* by A. E. Housman

Prologue

The rain which had been falling steadily from a sky that looked like a great canopy of deliquescent slate had begun to ease to a thin drizzle as I drove into Aylesbury, past the Royal Bucks Hospital and down Buckingham Street towards the town centre. At last I was beginning to recognize a few buildings, the fish and chip shop, and, a little further down, the pub where I had once spent a night with Sally. I turned into Kingsbury Square and took a left turn along a narrow street. Half-way down this I turned left again into the yard of the King's Head. I parked the car, took my bag from the boot and went into the hotel. The rain had almost stopped.

My room had two single beds, a wardrobe, a chest of drawers and a wash-basin with a mirror above it and a socket for an electric razor. I had noticed a bathroom on my way along the corridor. I unpacked my toilet-bag and some clean clothes. Then I went to the bathroom, bathed and put on fresh socks, underwear and shirt. Back in my room I looked at my watch. It was just after four o'clock. I had plenty of time to look around Aylesbury before dinner. Perhaps I would find an inviting restaurant that I could return to in the evening and where I would have more variety of choice and be given better food than the King's Head had to offer. I left the hotel and set off on foot to reacquaint myself with the town. The rain was no longer falling, though the sky was still a surly grey.

I had not been in Aylesbury for over forty years, nearly half a century.

The Market Square itself seemed almost unchanged. The statue of John Hampden looked towards the clock-tower in the centre, but the buildings that faced out onto the Square had changed a lot. Where I first lived when the family came to Aylesbury in 1931 was now a travel agency and, next to it, the offices of a building society. The Bull's Head, a fine half-timbered Tudor inn, had disappeared completely and in its place was the Hale Leys shopping centre. I walked down towards the town hall and on to the cattle market, but that, too, had gone and it was now a car-park. The old recreation ground had been built on with tall official-looking structures whose small dark windows gave nothing away. Only computers could live and work in places like those. I had expected Aylesbury to have changed, of course, but it was the manner of its change that troubled me with the beginnings of dejection. A more radical and complete transformation would have been more acceptable. The town centre at least was superficially unaltered; it was much as I had known it except for its submission to a kind of vulgarity, a seedy flashiness that had not been there before. It was the town I knew, but it had been violated, corrupted, betrayed.

The High Street was recognizable although the upper part, leading downhill from the Square, had been changed into a pedestrian precinct and none of the shops and offices that I had known was still there. In place of Page's, the baker and confectioner, and the little tobacconist and sweetshop where I used to spend my weekly pocket money of twopence in a single orgy of extravagance, buying perhaps a bar of Eton Toffee, a sherbet fountain and some chewing-gum, were a McDonald's hamburger joint, a Saucy Chef and a Deep Pan Pizza House. The Pavilion Cinema, or its shell, was still there, but it had become the Granada Luxury Bingo Centre. I carried on and found Highbridge Walk, the narrow path which led to the canal and had been a short cut on my journeys to school. This had changed scarcely at all except that the field on the right, just before the bridge, was fenced about and had become some kind of power station, and the terrace houses on the left looked smaller than I remembered them.

I crossed the bridge and walked away from the canal towards Queen's Park and my old school which looked almost unchanged though this, too, seemed to have shrunk a little. Behind the iron rails was the stone playground with the lavatories at one end and at the other, beneath the shelter of the shed roof, was the gate which had led to the forbidden territory of the girls' school. I stood for a few minutes staring at the grey building and the empty yard, waiting for something to happen, to be moved by remembered voices and faces, the ghosts of lost companions, recollected joys, fears, hopes and disappointments, but nothing came. The grey stone expanse remained empty. The building was silent. I turned and walked away, back into town but by another route, past King's Road where Doris once lived, and on to a road that led to the town centre. The Vale recreation ground seemed to be largely unchanged, except that it was almost empty. I went into the Vale, past the tennis courts to the field in which, at this time of the year, at least half a dozen improvised cricket matches would have been in progress but I saw only one solitary figure, wearing a white turban, bowling under-arm deliveries to a very small, dark-skinned boy who repeatedly stabbed awkwardly at the air with his toy bat after the ball had passed him.

Instead of going back to the main road into town I continued across the Vale on to Park Street and returned by a roughly circular route and found my way to Kingsbury Square, where we had lived in the flat above my father's photographic studio and shop after leaving the Market Square premises when I was eleven years old. This square, too, had retained its physical shape but, again, very few of the buildings were as I remembered them. Our own shop was now a health food store. The part of the Square which had served as the bus depot was no longer used for this purpose, and in place of the greengrocers, the music shop and corn-chandlers were now a Chinese takeaway, a computer centre and a Ladbroke's betting establishment. I walked along Pebble Lane to see that the County Non-Fiction Library, where I had spent many hours of delight and discovery, had become the premises of Burgess Office Equipment. St Mary's Church and Temple Street were not much changed but this area was quite deserted, as if it had been spared or overlooked by transmogrifying time and I felt like a ghost walking down the spectral, trafficless street, except that ghosts presumably do not suffer from physical fatigue, and I was beginning to wilt from my prolonged pounding of the pavements of Aylesbury. I returned to the King's Head and went to my room to lie on the bed and read, without deliberate irony, *Paradise Lost*, until it was time for dinner.

I had not seen any eating-place during my afternoon peregrination other than the untempting junk food joints so I decided to eat in the hotel restaurant. After an unspeakably dreadful meal I left the King's Head and again walked round Market Square. I went into the Crown and Bull, a new pub which had replaced the Bull's Head and the Crown Inn, and found myself in a dimly, yet infernally, lighted bar, malodorous with stale tobacco smoke and noisy with the beat and howl of juke-box pop. I turned round at once and returned to the street and set off back towards the King's Head. Just before I went into the hotel I heard yells and howls and the sound of running feet and, looking back, I saw a group of young men running across the other end of the square and I thought of Milton's "sons of Belial, flown with insolence and wine".

A few moments later I was sitting in the lounge bar with my pint of bitter and I remembered the place as it seemed to me when I first drank there, under the legal age for consuming alcohol and much impressed by the sophistication and stylishness of most of the customers. Now the only other drinkers in the place were a quartet of young office workers, perhaps in local government, who were gossiping about people and events connected with their work, and a couple of men whom I took to be reps of some kind who drank at the bar, speaking in low voices and periodically uttering loud barks and brayings of mirth. My depression deepened.

5

I remembered how, during the war when I had been stationed in the north of Scotland and, later, in the Middle East, I had cherished the memory of Aylesbury as a kind of amulet against despair, a dream of rural sweetness and light, an arcadian landscape in which music and poetry and the possibility of romantic love were ubiquitous presences. And, indeed, it really had been different from what it had now become. I was not deceiving myself when I recalled those summer days when my brother, Kenneth, and I would walk on the Chilterns above Wendover, reciting to each other the poems we had recently discovered, stopping for a lunch of bread and cheese and beer at the Leather Bottle and returning in the evening to this very place, the King's Head, for more beer and poetry. We had played cricket at Hartwell and, after the match, had drunk in The Bugle. The Whaddon Chase Hunt would meet in the Market Square and be supplied with stirrup-cups from the Bull's Head.

Aylesbury was then a small, quiet market town. It was less than an hour's journey by rail from London so, when Kenneth and I were in our teens we could go to a Promenade Concert at the Queen's Hall or to the Old Vic to see Gielgud in *Lear* or *The Tempest*; while Oxford was only half the distance of London and could be reached, and often was, by bicycle. Yes, Aylesbury had been a good, quiet place to live fifty years ago. So you might think my growing up there had been a small idyll, something to be looked back upon with affection, a dream of prelapsarian happiness? But it was not. My childhood and adolescence had not been at all like that, and suddenly I knew that the feeling of dejection which had begun to weigh on my spirits as soon as I had entered the outskirts of Aylesbury, and had deepened and darkened with every hour spent in the place, was not caused so much by the depredations and vulgarizations suffered by the town as by a hitherto unacknowledged recognition that, though the recollections of pleasure and excitement in a growing response to natural and artistic beauty were authentic, these experiences were brighter and more valued in recollection for having taken place against a background dark and heavy with fear, shame and hatred.

I had come to Aylesbury with the intention of staying for at least a few days but now I knew that I would leave the next morning. I would come back, but only in the mind, and I would try to relive some of those early experiences which, I suppose, had their part to play in making me into the man I was to become.

CHAPTER
ONE

We arrived in Aylesbury in 1931, my mother and father, my brother Kenneth, older than I by two years, and my sister, Sylvia, younger by five years. She was four and Kenneth was eleven. My parents, I suppose, were in their early thirties, my mother two or three years older than my father. He was called James Bain, his wife Elsie Mabel. I had been christened John Vernon but, for some reason that I've never understood, I was always called by my second name. When I discarded the name Bain fourteen years later I kept the Vernon, not because I liked the sound of it but because it had somehow become me. That's who I was and always had been and always would be. Getting rid of Bain didn't worry me at all. It was a relief. Ostensibly I changed it because I was on the run from the army, and needed to hide my identity, but I suspect that the real reason was because it was *his* name, my father's, the name of someone I had reason to detest. Stripping myself of his name and adopting one that had no connection with him was an act of symbolic dissociation. I wanted to get rid of the bastard. Just a few incidents from before our arrival in Aylesbury might give you some idea why this was so.

A very early memory: I was three years old and we were on the ship going from Liverpool to Dublin on a foolish and ill-fated expedition to Ballaghaderreen in Roscommon, where my father was to set up for a year or so as a photographer. When the ship was well out into the Irish Sea my father must have felt oppressed by the tedium of the journey for he decided to entertain himself, and possibly me, with one of his little jokes. He picked me up and carried me onto the boat deck where he held me over the rail with only the black waves below me, leaping, and foaming like enormous wolves, hungry for the proffered titbit. My shrieks were gratifyingly loud and were counterpointed by his wild laughter.

He was not entirely without humour, but his sense of the comic was not like that of anyone else I have ever known. The spectacle of someone's distress or pain, preferably though not necessarily caused by him, was the only thing that afforded him amusement. I now understand, and have understood for many years, that he was a sadist: I remember many instances of his grim pleasure derived from inflicting physical or mental pain on my brother or on me, but even today I am puzzled by those occasions when his victim's anguish, terror or disappointment excited not stern satisfaction but delighted laughter.

When the family had settled in Ballaghaderreen whatever expectations my father had entertained of making a tolerable living quickly foundered on the rocks of a general poverty which allowed little surplus money for indulging in the luxury of photographic

9

portraits. The few commissions to photograph wedding or school groups were sufficient only to keep the family supplied with barely adequate nourishment: our diet consisted almost exclusively of potatoes, porridge and soda-bread with the very rare additions of meat or fish and, even more infrequently, tinned pineapple chunks. The childhood treats of toffees, chocolate or any kind of confectionery were virtually unknown to Kenneth and me so we were rendered speechless with joy and anticipation when father called us from the back yard, where we had been playing, to come into the kitchen-living-room where he had placed on the table a half-pound slab of wrapped milk chocolate.

"All right," he said to Kenneth, "you open it. You can have half each."

Kenneth, who could scarcely believe that he was not dreaming, picked up the slab of chocolate and removed the shiny blue outer wrapping and paused before tearing off the silver paper.

"Go on!" father urged, clearly at least as excited as we were.

Kenneth tore off the silver paper. For a moment we both felt a sick incomprehension. The "chocolate" was made of wood. It was a shop-window display model of the real thing. Kenneth and I said nothing as we heard our father's prodigious laughter and saw his wild, excited eyes. For us it had been too good to be true anyway. So we went back to our play in the yard, refusing to show our disappointment, instinctively colluding to minimize his triumphant pleasure in our discomfiture. But we were never to forget.

His more straightforward brutality, the regular use of the "strap", was so much a part of childhood that specific occasions of punishment can be recalled only if there was some particular cause for their separation from the usual beatings, an unusual locus perhaps, a different punitive instrument, or a specially outrageous perversion of justice. One of the beatings I received in Ballaghaderreen falls into this last category. Quite simply I was wholly innocent of the crime of which I was accused, the stealing of some preserved fruit that was being kept either for parental consumption or a festive occasion. I had not taken the fruit. But my father chose not to believe my denials and I was whacked on the bare buttocks with the strap and, despite my howls, the punishment continued until I admitted, falsely, my guilt.

The strap was one of those leather strops on which cut-throat razors were honed but I do not recall this one being used for any other purpose than flagellation. It used to hang by its loop on a hook at the side of the fireplace, a permanent reminder of the consequences of misconduct and an important feature in the private imagery of early childhood. The first instance that I can remember of his cruelty being directed to someone other than his children also revealed another unpleasant aspect of his nature, a relishing of not simply the physical pain that his victim might suffer but also of any humiliation that might accompany or result from that pain, in other words the sly thrill of *schadenfreude*. This event occurred a couple of years or so after the wooden chocolate episode, when we were living in Beeston, near Nottingham, sharing a small terrace house on the Chilwell Road with my mother's parents.

I was about seven years old, certainly no more than that, yet I remember this little drama with undiminished vividness, and every detail is recalled, too, by my brother Kenneth, who shared, and still shares, with me the disgust and shame that was engendered by my father's behaviour. At that time our parents, unusually for them, sustained a friendship with a married couple, Bob and Dolly Linacre, who lived in Nottingham and had one child, a boy of about my age called Ivan. Dolly had been a schoolfriend of my mother's and my guess is that Bob endured rather than enjoyed whatever intimacy he was obliged to share with my father in order that his wife could continue the childhood friendship. He was a gentle and, I think, rather shy man who seemed contentedly dominated by his more robust and vivacious wife.

Kenneth and I had been given as a Christmas present a set of cheap and very crudely manufactured boxing gloves. The lumpy padding had, after brief use, worked its way from the knuckle part of each glove to the finger-tips so that little or no cushioning of the fist was afforded, and the outer cover was made of coarse cloth, instead of the soft leather of which the real thing would have been fashioned, so that even a light blow from someone wearing such a glove would be almost as painful as a thump on the nose from a bare fist. I do not know whether my father had ever boxed competitively. Certainly he had received some instruction on the basic moves, probably when he was undergoing his Army training during the First World War. I've no idea whether or not Bob Linacre had served in any branch of the armed forces but he gave no impression of being, or wishing to be, a fighting man of any kind.

Bob and Dolly, with their son Ivan, had come over from Nottingham to have Sunday tea with us. My grandparents were absent, perhaps visiting friends or relations. After the meal we were all in the small front room which was used only for the entertainment of guests, or on other festive occasions, when my father told Kenneth to fetch the boxing gloves. When my brother returned with them he and I were ordered to give an exhibition of our pugilistic skill. Kenneth, then aged nine, was a good deal taller and heavier than I but he was not the kind of child who would take advantage of these assets. In the quite narrow space between the front door which opened onto the pavement and the opposite door which led to the kitchen we swung away at each other, neither inflicting much damage on his opponent, until father called a halt. He was beginning to show signs of a dangerous excitement. Perhaps Ivan would like to have a go with Vernon, he suggested, a proposition that was promptly rejected by Dolly. Then what about Bob?

"Come on, Bob," he said, "get the gloves on! You and me!"

His guest, with some uneasy laughter and obvious embarrassment, declined the invitation. My father insisted. He had managed somehow to squeeze his hands into a pair of his children's boxing gloves and was now on his feet and it was clear that he would not accept Bob's refusal.

"Come on!" he urged. "Just a couple of minutes.

Come on, Bob! Get the gloves on! You're not scared, are you?"

Bob may or may not have been scared. Most certainly he was dreadfully uncomfortable. Young as I was, I recognized and could sympathize with his embarrassment. His complexion reddened, as if from too close proximity to a fire, and his attempt at a smile made him look more aghast than amused. So, with reluctance, but not, I think, with fear, for surely he would have thought there were no grounds for it, he allowed himself to be persuaded to remove his jacket and put on the boxing gloves. My father was waiting, shirt-sleeves rolled up, eager, eyes bulging with anticipatory pleasure, his mouth fixed in the peculiar half-grin, half-snarl, that Kenneth and I had come to recognize as a danger signal. His back was against the front door. Bob approached him, still with that uncertain smile that was contradicted by the expression in his eyes of dawning understanding and apprehension.

"Touch gloves," my father said.

Bob extended his gloved hands tentatively. My father tapped them with his own and adopted a threatening stance. Bob retreated. His own fists were raised in front of his face for protective rather than hostile purposes. I knew that something dreadful was going to happen. It did. My father moved forward until Bob's back was against the kitchen door; then it began. He knocked Bob's gloves to one side with his left hand and drove his right into Bob's face and followed up with three or four blows delivered with full force and all the time that snarling and self-congratulatory grin was unchanged but his eyes grew wilder with delight and satisfaction.

Dolly was crying out her protestations and even my mother found the courage to call, "No, Jim! No!"

Bob's nose was bleeding and he crouched against the door trying, without much success, to protect himself from the next attack. He looked like the terrified and humiliated victim of a playground bully. His son, Ivan, looked on, staring eyes, pale and frightened. Dolly rose to intercede. My mother called out again for her husband to desist. He stepped back, the mad grin still in place. "What's up?" he said. "Just a bit of fun. That right, Bob? Just a bit of fun."

I swear that he was expecting admiration of his strength and prowess. What I felt was disgust and shame and hatred. Until then I think that I had known nothing but a simple fear of him. Now I hated him. I was afraid of him, too, but from then onward hatred was the more powerful emotion — even though I was no older than seven — and it would survive long after fear had lost its potency.

To Aylesbury, then, in the autumn of 1931: the first photographic business that my father established there was in the Market Square. There was no shop-front. An open doorway led from the pavement into a narrow hall, and glass-fronted showcases on either wall contained examples of my father's work, portraits of children and their parents, of dogs and wedding groups. At the top of the first flight of stairs was the reception area and studio and, above that, the dark-room where the processing of the negatives took place and, higher still in this tall narrow building, the family's limited living-quarters. Kenneth and I slept in a small room which was only just large enough to admit the three-quarter-size bed that we shared. My mother, father, and four-year-old sister, Sylvia, slept in the other bedroom, and meals were cooked and eaten in the only other room, though the studio could be adapted as extra sleeping accommodation on the rare occasions that visitors came to stay.

Kenneth and I attended Queen's Park Boys' School. In those days English schools were divided broadly into the three groups of elementary, secondary and the private fee-charging schools with their independent foundations and governing bodies, the most expensive and famous of which, to the understandable confusion of people from other countries, were called public schools. The term "secondary" applied to the grammar schools which charged relatively small fees and had traditionally been established for the "trading classes" and did not accommodate boarders; whereas the public schools were for the "governing classes" and most of their pupils and virtually all of the staff lived on the premises during term. After the Board of Education's Consultative Committee published their Hadow Report in 1926 a limited number of children from the elementary schools were given "scholarships" to the grammar schools at the age of eleven, their promotion being determined by a compulsory examination. Not all of the grammar schools were willing to accept working-class children and a number of them transformed themselves into public schools by getting rid of their Scout Troops or Boys' Brigade Companies and establishing in their place Officers' Training Corps, and contriving to get their headmasters elected to sit on the National Headmasters' Conference, thus gaining public school status, whether or not their pupils were boarders.

Queen's Park was an elementary school. Kenneth had recently been successful in the scholarship examination and had been awarded a place at a grammar school in Nottingham but this award was not, it seemed, transferable to Buckinghamshire, so he accompanied me to our new school. This one was neither better nor worse than most schools of its kind. It was small, holding about two hundred and fifty children who were divided into seven classes which were known as "standards". I was in Standard Three, Kenneth in Standard Five.

The building was a simple, rectangular, one-storeyed structure. As you entered the iron gate into the stone playground you would turn right to enter the junior part of the school, and left if you were in Standard Four or above. At one end was the senior cloakroom and two classrooms; at the other, the same facilities for the juniors. In between was the school hall with a rostrum at one end, at the side of which stood an upright piano, and the doors to the three intermediate classrooms were on your right as you faced the rostrum. The Headmaster's study was a small balcony room above the rostrum and it was reached by a flight of stairs next to the junior cloakroom. If you went out of the junior exit you would find, at that end of the playground, a long shelter supplied by a tiled roof sloping down from the wall, which separated us from the girls' school, and supported by metal poles which were painted green. There was a gate at one end of the wall and this led into the forbidden territory of the girls' playground; at the other end of the wall was the workshop in which carpentry was taught once a week to the seniors, that is, to boys aged twelve and above. At the end of the playground opposite to the shelter were the brick walls of the lavatories.

Kenneth and I walked the three-quarters of a mile or so from Market Square to school each weekday morning to arrive there before nine o'clock when everyone assembled for prayers, hymn-singing and homilies, warnings and exhortations from the Headmaster. In theory, and I suppose sometimes in practice, he was called Mr Little, but in private he was always referred to by the boys as Nap, which was short for Napoleon. It was not difficult to see why this sobriquet had been bestowed on him. He was very short and rather stout and his thinning hair curled wispily onto his forehead in a way reminiscent of portraits of Bonaparte, but there were other reasons for the appositeness of the nickname. It was clear, even to us children, that he was a man who took pleasure in the exercise and display of power, and we sensed, too, that he suffered from delusions of grandeur and that he was a comic, perhaps slightly pathetic figure. I don't think he was at all unpleasant but he was absurd in his strutting complacency and his outrageous boastfulness.

He had written a series of textbooks the subject-matter of which, as far as I recall, anticipated the "combined social studies" that were to become an orthodox part of the curricula in the schools of a considerably later period. I seem to remember an account of the ways in which local government operated; a chapter on simple economics in which the difference between wealth and money was explained; something about town-planning, and a section on the National Grid, and so on. There were some rather indistinct photographic illustrations and line-drawings of no great accomplishment. My recollections of the books' contents are vague but the feeling of boredom that they generated comes back quite strongly. These textbooks were used throughout the school and Nap would go from classroom to classroom to make sure that the pupils were in no doubt as to the value of these works nor as to the distinction of their author. When, about a year after our arrival at the school, Nap left to take up another post, or — less likely perhaps — to make authorship his sole occupation, his textbooks disappeared, without comment from our teachers, from the syllabus and, as far as I know, from the premises.

Nap was replaced by a Mr Jones, a choleric little man with large projecting teeth, whose frequent fulminations were delivered with a fine spray of saliva. No nickname was ever bestowed on him and this now suggests to me that the usually jocular renaming of figures in authority only occurs when the recipients are the objects of affection or perhaps admiration. I don't think any of us admired Nap but there was, we felt, something likeable about him, something innocent about the exuberance of his swank that pleased us. Almost all of the other teachers were known by nicknames. There was "Toss" Plested who played soccer and cricket for the town first elevens and was in charge of the school teams, a responsibility which he carried out with great humour and sacrifice of much of his spare time. I can't remember, if indeed I ever knew, why he was called "Toss", though I guess that it was something to do with legendary luck, good or ill, in spinning the coin preceding a cricket or football match. "Dabber" Dean was a lean, bald man, a keen geographer, who, for reasons that I have never understood, inspired a kind of awe that contained something of pure fear, in all the boys, even the most recalcitrant. He was the only teacher who never had to raise his voice or issue threats of punishment in order to keep his class silent and attentive. Why we named him "Dabber", apart from the alliterative effect, I never knew.

"Pete" Dawson was a small stout elderly man who wore gold-rimmed glasses and a moustache with waxed points. I don't think he was specially popular or unpopular; the only thing I clearly remember about him was that, on each Armistice Day, when a special assembly was held in the school hall, during the two minutes' silence "Pete" was always to be seen wiping away a fugitive tear, shed — so rumour had it — in memory of his son who had been killed in France. If "Pete" had, at this time, been about sixty, and I'm by no means sure that he was as old as this, though he seemed a lot older than most of the other teachers, it is chronologically quite possible that he could have been the father of a son who had perished in the Great War. True or not, the story made him somehow more sympathetic to us than otherwise we would have found him. Whether the "Pete" was a diminutive of his true Christian name or taken from some mythical comic figure such as Mexican Pete or Piccolo Pete I do not know.

20

There was another teacher at Queen's Park whose nickname was a diminutive of a full Christian name, "Archie" Dormer, but I shall write more about him later because he was the most interesting and likeable of my teachers and the only one who gave me positive encouragement in my reading and fledgling attempts to become a writer.

The teacher who was in charge of Standard Three in that autumn of 1931 was Mr Gunstone, never referred to by any nickname, though the "Mr" was always dropped when we spoke of him among ourselves. For reasons which I could not understand then, and have never since been able to explain to myself, he was the butt for the taunts and tricks of generations of boys over whom he seemed quite incapable of exercising control. It was a tradition to "play him up" and we must have made his life a torment, but there was no obvious reason why he should have been elected to fulfil this role. He was not physically unimposing nor was his behaviour in any way eccentric. In fact he was a strongly built, rather athletic-looking man, of above average height, dark-haired and quite good-looking in a regular-featured, decidedly masculine way. One of his additional duties was to conduct classes in life-saving and take charge of swimming throughout the school, and while he was not a spectacular aquatic performer he was still young and fit enough to go into the water.

Another strange aspect of his inability to control the boys in his care was his readiness to use the cane and to use it with agonizing vigour and accuracy. I am quite sure that he caned more boys in a week than Dabber

Dean or Archie Dormer caned in a term, or longer, but — and there are instructive wider sociological and psychological implications here — his resorting so frequently to corporal punishment seemed to have no deterrent effect at all on the anarchic behaviour of his pupils. I do not believe for a moment that he derived any pleasure from inflicting pain on the young malefactors; his use and over-use of the cane were caused by a kind of panic of desperation and impotence. On one occasion, when no one would confess to having thrown the apple core which had been flung at his head when his back was turned as he wrote on the black board, he delivered six strokes of the cane, three on each hand, to every one of the thirty-six boys in the class. Half-way through the execution of this punishment he paused to remove his jacket and, at the end, he seemed to be exhausted. Those boys who were not especially ill-behaved or rebellious but who were afraid to reveal the identity of the real culprit tucked their burning hands under their armpits, tried, not always successfully, to hold back the tears, and muttered threats of telling their dads. Even at the time I was puzzled by his failure to control us and, while I was as much responsible as anyone for making his life miserable, I was aware of a sly undercurrent of guilt beneath the excitement and hilarity that our antics and his reactions afforded us.

Kenneth and I saw little of each other during school hours; his two years' seniority separated us at that time and place in ways difficult to bridge. We were at physically different ends of the school and he found friends among his coevals who would not have welcomed my company. He was cleverer than I, almost invariably top of his class, and he was good at ball games, especially cricket, at which he played for the school in the season following our arrival at Queen's Park. We were quite close at home in our shared fear and hatred of "him", or "the Old Man", as we now referred to our father, but the common interest in books and music that would soon narrow the chronological gap had not yet defined itself. So for the next year or so we spent at least as much of our leisure time apart as together.

My closest friend at school was Eddie MacSweeney. He was a few months older than I, though we were in the same class. Whatever the basis of this friendship, it was not founded on similarities of temperament or on mutual interests. Eddie was reckless, with an almost crazy compulsion to put himself in unnecessary danger; to him no tree was unclimbable, the ice of no frozen pond too thin to slide upon, no height too great to dive from and no one in authority too forbidding to provoke. He would accept any "dare". On one cold day in November he and I, with another boy, called Hedley Horwood, were walking along the tow-path of the canal when Horwood boasted that he had swum in Halton Reservoir in April when no one else would venture into the freezing water.

"That's nothing," Eddie said. "I've been swimming in the cut when there was snow on the ground."

"Liar!"

"Not!"

"Y'are!"

"All right," said Horwood. "I dare you go in now."

Without hesitation Eddie took off his clothes, plunged into the canal, swam half-way across, turned and came back and scrambled out onto the tow-path. He tried to say something but his teeth were chattering so violently that speech was impossible. His face and body were dyed by the cold an alarming stormy blue and his limbs were trembling and jerking as if electric charges were running through them. He managed to grasp his jersey and shirt in agued hands and started to rub himself with them until he was dry enough to get dressed. He was soon laughing and assuring us that he felt marvellous after his little swim and he wouldn't mind going in again. I was relieved when Horwood didn't challenge him to do so because Eddie would almost certainly have stripped and again dived into the icy water.

He was one of six children, though the three younger siblings had been fathered by Mrs MacSweeney's second husband, Mr Welch, a small morose man, who was a road sweeper for the council, and these children had taken his name. Eddie's older brother, Charlie, had left school and he straddled, heroically, a Brough Superior motor-cycle, and was too grown-up to take much notice of Eddie and me; Kathleen was in her last year at Queen's Park Girls' School and she too showed little interest in the activities and antics of her younger brother and his friend. Eddie's own attitude to the Welch stepsister and two brothers was one of contemptuous hostility which I could not, at the time, understand, though it seems obvious now that it originated from jealous resentment at his mother's betrayal of his dead father in marrying, and becoming mother to the children of, Mr Welch.

Eddie was agile, acrobatic rather than athletic, and formal games held little attraction for him. He had a flat, rather simian face, with big, projecting teeth and he seemed always to be cheerful. He took no pleasure in reading, not even comics, and viewed my enjoyment of books with slightly puzzled and tolerant amusement. I took him home a couple of times but my mother thought he was "common" and the Old Man said that he didn't want that little guttersnipe in the house again and I was to avoid his company in future. What drew me to Eddie was his enjoyment of the absurdity of the authoritarian world, his gusto for physical adventure and his generosity. The Old Man's disapproval of him was an additional seal on the friendship.

Like most friendships of prepubescence and early adolescence, mine with Eddie was ardent and often stormy. We would quite frequently quarrel over some real or imagined betrayal or, perhaps more often, because we were bored and had nothing more interesting to do. For a few days after such a dispute, each of us would appear to have formed a close partnership with another boy, and the new alliance would be flaunted almost coquettishly in front of the other with extravagant displays of satisfaction with and devotion to the new companion, who would be more or less ruthlessly cast aside when the inevitable reconciliation occurred. That we should never be reunited after one of these quarrels was unthinkable. It seemed that we were in some way necessary to each other.

I don't think I really liked Eddie or, if I did, it was a liking that was qualified by a number of reservations. I found some of his physical habits repugnant. When we shared food or ate together, as we often did when we picnicked in summer by the canal or on the banks of Halton Reservoir, I could not bear to watch or listen to him as he ate. He gobbled his food with the same eagerness and disregard for decorum that he showed when engaging in other pleasurable activities. I'm sure that Eddie, had he known of it, would have been bewildered by this revulsion as I am sure that there were features of my behaviour and personality that Eddie found unpleasant, but each of us, unless provoked by some outrageous hostile or treacherous act of the other's, would be careful not to reveal and use as ammunition those aspects of his "best friend's" personality and conduct that he disliked.

I was sometimes irritated by Eddie's philistinism, not only by his lack of imagination but by his impatience and scorn for any values other than materialistic ones. When in the early darkness of autumn nights we went scrumping in the orchards of the posh houses on the northern outskirts of Aylesbury I secretly dramatized the expeditions and derived at least as much enjoyment from the heroic fantasy I was elaborating as from the juiciness of the apples we had stolen. But I knew better than to allow Eddie to suspect that I was acting in an interior drama and furthermore that he had been allotted his role and was unconsciously playing his part, a subordinate one to mine of course. So our friendship continued, with some deceit on my side, and it would endure during the four years until Eddie left school, a few months before it was my turn to leave. His first job was as delivery boy for the Co-op bakery and I would sometimes see him jumping down from the horse-drawn van with a huge basket of loaves and he would advertise his presence with yodelling cries. We met a few times after I had left school but the old friendship had somehow evaporated and we found that we were slightly uncomfortable and almost formal in our dealings with each other.

Not long before the family left Beeston to come to Aylesbury my maternal grandmother died, and I guess that she must have left my mother and father a little money to enable them to set up the photographic business in Market Square. This was the beginning of what was to become a time of relative prosperity. A few miles from Aylesbury was the RAF station, Halton Camp, where apprentice aircraftmen were trained, and many of the young recruits, proud of their new uniforms, came to be photographed; these customers supplied the small but solid foundation on which to build what was to become a modestly flourishing concern. The Old Man had learnt his trade gradually over the previous ten years, working as a beach photographer in Skegness during the holiday season and being taught the skills of retouching, developing and printing in a studio owned by a relation of my mother.

The success of the business kept both parents very busy, for my mother was proficient in colouring, retouching, trimming and mounting the finished photographs. Kenneth and I were left to look after our little sister for quite long periods and on Saturdays, when there was no school, my regular task was to take Sylvia out just after breakfast with instructions not to return until dinner time. Quite often, and understandably, she would become fretful and tired after three hours or so of trailing along the canal tow-path or playing on the swings in the old recreation ground and when cajoling and patience failed to silence her howls I would resort to threats and imprecations. These, of course, did nothing to quieten her dismal wailing and ensured a thrashing for me when, on our return, she reported that I had shouted at her and been nasty.

I have no idea why, or by what agency, my mother was converted to that quasi-religion called Christian Science, but converted she was, and this meant that Kenneth and I were sent out every Sunday afternoon to the Girl Guides' Hall which became, on the Sabbath, the Christian Science Sunday School and church. There, a dozen or so children were separated into junior and senior groups and each one sat in a semicircle to be instructed in the doctrines of the faith by well-meaning but self-deluded ladies. The place smelled of piety, a mélange of the perfume worn by Miss Britten and Miss Wooleston, the fresh flowers which they always brought to relieve the drabness of our surroundings, and another, vaguely yeasty smell which came from the pages of our Bibles and copies of *Science and Health, with Key to the Scriptures* by Mary Baker Eddy.

Mrs Eddy, a wealthy and much married American, founded her sect in the second half of the nineteenth century. Her followers were to read the Bible regularly but only in conjunction with *Science and Health*, which explained the significance of the biblical texts. Very broadly, Christian Science stated that all evil was unreal, that sickness, pain, fear and poverty were illusions proceeding from "error", or wrong thinking. Since we were made in God's image it followed that any imperfection, physical or metaphysical, could not be real. "Miraculous" cures had been accomplished by good Christian Scientists refusing to admit error into their minds. Apparently the more orthodox believers in sin and redemption through the suffering of Christ had got it all wrong. "The way to escape the misery of sin is to cease sinning," wrote Mrs Eddy. This was a religion for the healthy and the well-heeled.

So every Sunday afternoon my little group sat and listened in the scented gloom to Miss Wooleston sweetly expounding these preposterous doctrines, and it did not occur to any of us to question them. *Science and Health* was bound, like the Bibles, in soft morocco with gold tooling and with the same flimsy pages and faint bready odour, the scent of holiness. Its contents could not be anything but true. So I felt not only bored and resentful of the waste of time which I could have spent enjoyably, but guilty too. And when in the summer of 1932 I was afflicted with boils on my neck the physical pain was not diminished by the knowledge that these excrescences were the result of my own "error". Of course, as a Christian Scientist, I did not see a doctor, though my mother deviated from absolute faith in the unreality of sickness and the wicked folly of treating physical ailments with medical remedies when she applied a hot bread-poultice to the boils.

My mother seems an unlikely proselyte to such an

eccentric religion, or any kind for that matter, and I have never understood what drew her to it or what kept her allegiance firm. She spent quite a lot of her leisure time in reading, but the books she read were mainly popular middle- to low-brow novels by such authors as Warwick Deeping, Naomi Jacob, and Cecil Roberts, and she appeared to possess no intellectual curiosity at all. But, then, at the age of ten, I accepted most adult behaviour as being beyond my understanding. My mother, whom we always called Mam, as was customary in the North Midlands, had always seemed the embodiment of quiet gentleness. She did not use the strap on us. She rarely raised her voice. The fact that she never showed any sign of positive affection for either Kenneth or me was not a cause for distress. This was the way things were. The idea of her embracing us, or — horrific notion — *kissing* us, was too embarrassingly awful to be contemplated. When Dolly Linacre, who was a demonstrative mother, cuddled and kissed her son Ivan, Kenneth and I were genuinely shocked as if we had witnessed something obscene. No wonder we considered Ivan to be a sissy. Also, and this was the final proof of his sissiness, he wore underpants. Perhaps I should explain.

The Old Man did not wear and never had worn, this shameful garment. He boasted of this more than once as proof of his incontestable manliness. Only sissies wore underpants. And Kenneth and I really believed this to be true, right up until the time when we joined the army and were issued with these articles and found, to our surprise, that they were worn by everyone, including men whose masculinity could not be doubted.

Kenneth and I made the journey to school and back to Market Square twice a day, for there were no school dinners in those days, and like all the boys at Queen's Park, we had to go home for our midday meal. School itself was bearable but hardly inspiring. By the end of 1932 I was in Standard Five, Pete Dawson's class, and Kenneth was in Standard Seven and being taught by Archie Dormer. Pete, who was quite a lot older than the rest of the teachers, was, I suspect, a tired and disappointed man whose vocation, if ever he would have claimed to have received such a thing, had long since been silenced by the repetitive dreariness of the job. He seemed content to get through each day with as little trouble as possible from his pupils whom he regarded with resigned distaste. Each teacher was responsible for instructing his class in the main subjects of arithmetic and English grammar and composition. Dabber Dean would come into the class once a week to teach geography, and Toss Plested taught us art and history. My performance in all these subjects, except for English, was mediocre, but I found the composition lessons enjoyable even though Pete chose unexciting subjects for us to write on — "A Day in the Life of a Postman", "A Windy Day", "My Favourite Hobby", "An Ideal Holiday", and so forth. I think I showed some ingenuity in concocting stories of high adventure under such titles, and Pete did not object to these, though his acceptance was more likely to have been caused by apathy than appreciation of my imaginative powers.

My writing was not confined to school composition lessons. When not engaged in outdoor pursuits I spent virtually all of my spare time either writing or reading. My literary tastes were, at the age of ten, quite comprehensive. The only books in the home, apart from Mam's library novels, were a set of Scott's Waverley novels, a large illustrated *Pilgrim's Progress*, possessions left by my maternal grandfather, the Bible and *Science and Health*. I had managed to get through *Ivanhoe* but the only other Scott novel I attempted, *The Black Dwarf of Montrose*, defeated me. Kenneth had been lent or given copies of *The Four Just Men* and *The Green Archer*, both by Edgar Wallace, and I read these with enjoyment. What I got the greatest pleasure from at that time were the "public school" stories in the weekly *Magnet*, in which Billy Bunter and Harry Wharton of the "Famous Five" appeared. A classmate called Roy Coveney bought the *Magnet* every week and he handed his copies on to me when he had read them. I got hold of *Tom Brown's Schooldays* around that time and enjoyed it, but not so much as the *Magnet* stories.

It was a year or eighteen months later that I began to read the same books as Kenneth. We both found P. G. Wodehouse irresistibly funny, and the Old Man, who hated to see us reading anything, was especially enraged by our chuckles as we followed the exploits of Psmith or Ukridge or Bertie Wooster. A different kind of pleasure was found in John Buchan's novels of adventure and espionage, and we enjoyed another, softer kind of romanticism in the stories of a writer called Maurice Walsh who is — probably deservedly — quite forgotten today. I first read *David Copperfield* at this time and began to respond to something in Dickens that was not simply a matter of being implicated in the narrative and compelled to read on from a fever to know what was going to happen next, though it could not be separated from these. I would go back and again read certain passages — David's first arrival at Betsey Trotwood's cottage was one — simply for the pleasure that the language gave me, a physical enjoyment of the weight and taste and texture of the words. I did not know it, of course, but I was responding to the poetic quality in Dickens's prose.

As for poetry itself I had not yet found my way to a conscious liking of it, partly because of the complete lack of any kind of guidance. Pete Dawson did not ignore it, but his use of it in the classroom was not likely to inspire in any of his pupils a love of the art. He used the tattered and ink-stained set of anthologies as apparatus for training the memory. This book contained a rather peculiar mixture of traditional anthology pieces by Gray, Wordsworth, Keats and Tennyson; a few "modern" poets such as G. K. Chesterton, John Drinkwater and Sir Henry Newbolt, and a long-winded piece of whimsy entitled "Miss Thompson Goes Shopping" by someone called Martin Armstrong, chunks of which we were set to learn by heart. Another use for the anthology was the punitive one of setting miscreants to copy out verses in their best handwriting. Yet, despite Pete's efforts to instil a robust dislike of poetry in his young students, I found that some of the poems that I came across when I browsed through the class anthology were, in a way that I could not have explained, disturbing and insistently memorable.

Some of these poems were not in the least difficult to

understand. J. C. Squire's sonnet beginning "There was an Indian, who had known no change . . ." pleased me, especially the last two lines:

Columbus's doom-burdened caravels
Slant to the shore, and all their seamen land.

I was much taken, too, with a poem by Sir Henry Newbolt called "He Fell among Thieves" in which an unnamed British officer of some kind is sentenced to death by his savage captors, also unidentified. I preferred this poem to the more famous "Vitai Lampada", finding, even at the age of ten or eleven, that "voice of a schoolboy" exhorting the hard-pressed soldiery to "Play up! play up! and play the game!" not quite believable. But the poem which cast a real spell over me was, apart from the first five lines, quite incomprehensible; and years later, when I first came across T. S. Eliot's observation that poetry can communicate before it is understood, I remembered my finding Wordsworth's sonnet, "It is a Beauteous Evening, Calm and Free", as perplexing as it was haunting.

We did not possess at home a radio, or wireless as it was then called, so the only distraction from the fairly grim present was through reading and, for me, writing. I filled the whole of a Woolworth exercise-book with a story called "The Green Army". A band of outlaws roamed the forest bringing succour to the oppressed poor and retribution to the villainous rich. I was not at all clear about the historical period in which these events occurred and, if questioned about this, I would

34

probably say that my story was set in "the olden days". After reading Edgar Wallace I turned to a modern setting and wrote a series of murders at the scenes of which the perpetrator of the crimes left his mocking visiting-card bearing a drawing of a black cat. These crimes remained unsolved because I lost interest in the underworld when I read Harrison Ainsworth's *Old St Paul's* and at once started on a historical romance which again was set in those unspecific olden days.

The Old Man took no interest in my literary activities, indeed neither parent seemed to have much time to spend on the children. The business was evidently doing well and, as the Christmas of 1932 approached, both parents were kept so busy that we saw them only briefly over hurriedly prepared meals. A couple of days before Christmas, Mam said, "Have you decided what you want for your presents?"

I wanted a bicycle but I knew there was no hope of getting one. Neither Kenneth nor I was able to say.

"All right," Mam said. "I'll give you five shillings each and you can buy your own presents."

Perhaps it wasn't her fault, for they really were very busy finishing the portraits and family groups that had been ordered for Christmas, but I felt that she could have done better than this. So that evening, while the shops were still open, Kenneth and I set off, each with his two half-crowns, to find something to spend them on. It was a cold night and the pavements were crowded. The smell of excitement and extravagance was in the air, cigar smoke, loud voices laughing and calling out "Merry Christmas!". The lit windows of the shops were decorated with cotton-wool snow, tinsel and holly. Neither of us knew what to buy. After an hour of indecision I bought a little train set, a locomotive and two carriages and rails which when fitted together made a circular track of about eighteen inches in diameter. I chose it in a kind of panic of uncertainty, seduced by its shining newness. I knew as soon as I was handed the parcel that I did not really want it. Kenneth, more prudently, bought a novel called *Mr Perrin and Mr Traill* by Hugh Walpole and pocketed the one shilling and sixpence change. We went back to Market Square, to the dingy and musty flat which was always redolent of cats' piss. Our Christmas was not going to be a merry one but, though we did not know it then, it would be the last spent in that place for, in the following spring, when I was eleven, we moved to new premises, a shop and studio with living accommodation upstairs, in Kingsbury Square.

CHAPTER
TWO

The Kingsbury Square premises were newly built and seemed at first to be excitingly clean and well-lit and comparatively roomy. There were double shop-windows, behind which examples of the Old Man's work were displayed, photographs of babies and young children, family groups, portraits of individual men and women, dogs, brides and grooms and bridesmaids, and between the two windows was the door to the shop, or reception area, the only entrance to the building. You went from the pavement through this door and there, on your right, was a desk at which appointments or enquiries could be made. Facing you was the heavily curtained area, furnished as a studio with a divan, an upright, rather intricately carved oak chair for the individual sitter to perch on, powerful overhead adjustable lights and the old-fashioned camera on its tripod. Next to the studio was a staircase leading up to the flat above the shop. At the top of the stairs was a very small kitchen and a rear living-and-dining room which, as the business progressed, was used more and more as a work place until it was taken over entirely, and the front room, overlooking the Square, originally intended as a sitting-room, became the place where we lived and ate. At the back, the workroom had a door which led out onto a wooden landing and steps leading down to a back yard in which there was a small coal-bunker and a red brick shed with corrugated-iron roof, which served as the Old Man's dark-room. Here he did his developing and printing and enlarging. Back inside the main building, another flight of stairs led to a second floor on which there was a bathroom and lavatory and two bedrooms. Kenneth and I shared the rear one, still sleeping in the same bed, and Sylvia and my parents slept in the front bedroom.

We, the boys, did not have much furniture in our room. Apart from the bed there was a cane chair on which we could drape our clothes at night and a chest of drawers, but, despite its cheerlessness I spent there many hours of contentment, if not positive happiness, when I could sneak off, undetected by the Old Man, to lie on the bed and read a book or begin to write yet another abortive tale of adventure, whose period and setting would be determined by those of the story I was currently reading or had just finished.

The Old Man's aversion to our reading was accepted by Kenneth and me as yet another aspect of his commitment to making our lives as unpleasant as possible. It was obvious to us, young as we were, that he mistrusted, even hated, books as instruments of emasculation. "No wonder you're so soft! No wonder you've got spots!" he would cry. "Put that book down and get outside. Go and chop some trees down!" This exhortation to deforest the landscape was issued quite frequently and after our first mild perplexity, since he must have known there were no trees in Kingsbury Square and we possessed neither the skills nor the tools of lumberjacks, we assumed the command was some kind of metaphor or simply further evidence of his doubtful sanity. The only reading matter to receive his grudging approval and even interest took the form of pulp magazines of American origin dealing with the subject of boxing. These publications, with titles like *The Ring* and *Fight Stories* were acquired either by the "swapping" process, which was conducted keenly among our more literate schoolfriends and acquaintances, or they were bought in the twice-weekly market from the stall that specialized in selling cheap secondhand comics and magazines.

Both Kenneth and I were drawn more to the factual and historic contents of *The Ring* than the fiction of *Fight Stories*, for we quickly discovered that the true events of famous boxers' usually brief lives were far more dramatic and compelling than any pulp fiction could hope to be. Such pictorial illustrations as *Fight Stories* offered were crude line-drawings, but each issue of *The Ring* contained photographs of historic encounters, starkly black and white, the often spotted and blurred quality of these rough-grained reproductions lending a kind of authenticity to their witness that smoother, clearer pictures might not have possessed. It was from reading accounts of epic contests of the past and from long poring over those pictures of frozen violence, the ring with its thin taut ropes, the white canvas on which one of the fighters would often be depicted as sprawling while his triumphant opponent moved to a neutral corner and the dicky-bowed referee began, with upraised right hand, to chop away the ten defeating seconds, it was from those that a lifelong fascination with the mythology of the fight game developed.

The Old Man's interest in boxing was, I soon began to learn, quite different from ours. For a start it was much more chauvinistic. It was not simply British fighters who received his enthusiastic support but preferably British fighters from his own part of the country. He would become almost feverishly excited when a well-known boxer from Lancashire, especially if he came from Salford or Manchester, was taking part in a contest of importance.

We had been living in Kingsbury Square for a little more than a year and the family fortunes must have been improving for we had just bought our first wireless set. A boxer called Jackie Brown, a Manchester flyweight, had recently won the world title on a knock-out over a Tunisian, Young Perez, and the Old Man's sense of triumph was so intense that it would have been difficult for an observer to understand that he had not personally received some material gain from Brown's victory, indeed his delight could have scarcely been greater had he himself won the title. While Jackie Brown and the Old Man were enjoying the power and the glory conferred by the winning of a world Championship, a young Glaswegian flyweight named Benny Lynch was building a reputation as a devastating puncher and skilful ring tactician. Lynch and Brown were matched for the World title.

There was great excitement at Kingsbury Square over the forthcoming contest. The Old Man, of course, was totally convinced that he, or his representative, Jackie Brown, would teach the young Scottish pretender a quick and painful lesson.

"He won't last two rounds," said the Old Man. "Jackie will box rings round him and knock him out."

Neither of us had seen either of the boxers in action. However, I had read about Lynch in *Boxing News* and I knew that his record was unblemished.

I said, "I think Lynch will win."

The Old Man's laughter was loud and contemptuous.

"Jackie Brown is a brilliant box-fighter. This Glasgow corner-boy doesn't stand a chance!"

On the night of the fight I was not allowed to stay up to listen to the commentary on the wireless. The next morning I rose at seven-thirty and performed my daily task of sweeping the pavement in front of the shop and cleaning the windows. I then went upstairs for my breakfast.

The Old Man was sitting with my mother at the table over a cup of tea, smoking a Craven A cork-tipped cigarette. Before I sat down I said, "Who won? What happened?"

He looked at me balefully but said nothing.

"Who won the fight? Last night. Lynch and Brown. Who won?"

He said, and his lips barely moved, "Lynch."

"Lynch won? How? Points? A knock-out? How did he win?"

Again he took time over answering. Then he snapped "Knock-out. Second round. It was a fluke."

I was jubilant. "Second round! I told you he'd win!"

Two seconds later I was lying on my back blinking up at the ceiling. I felt as if a large rock had been flung into my face. I was dizzy and I could taste the warm saltiness of blood. I sat up and slowly began to climb to my feet. The Old Man had gone out of the room.

My mother said, "You shouldn't have taunted him. You might have known."

I was crying, not with pain so much as indignation. I was outraged. He had punched me as hard as he was able, a pile-driving straight right to the chin, because I had said that Lynch would win and I had been right.

I suppose he was then just past his mid-thirties. I was twelve years old.

Years later, when I had children of my own, I found myself puzzling over the Old Man's treatment of his sons, wondering what deep and powerful disappointment and resentment could have impelled him to behave with such violence and apparent loathing. His detestation of our reading anything other than the popular literature of boxing I began to suspect originated in a suspicion and hatred of the unknown places to which we could escape and he could not follow. When, in late 1933 or early 1934 Kenneth and I joined the Aylesbury and District Boxing Club he not only encouraged us to become members but almost uncomplainingly paid our subscriptions, though we quickly discovered that there was an impediment to any enjoyment we might have derived from our activities at the club.

Training nights were held once a week and he always attended these. Kenneth and I would arrive at the Castle

Street Hall which, for that night, had been transformed into a gymnasium with two ground-level, single-roped sparring rings, a heavy punch-bag, speed-ball and skipping ropes, and we would go into the dressing-room at the back of the hall and change into our gym-shorts, singlets and tennis shoes (proper boxing gear was to be acquired much later) and return to the gym to skip, punch the bag or perform ground exercises aimed at developing the abdominal muscles, until it was time to put on the gloves and go into the ring to spar for three one-and-a-half-minute rounds. And all the time we were both aware of the Old Man standing, always alone, never speaking to the few other spectators or club officials and watching us with an expression that we knew so well but could never confidently interpret, a faint smirk, almost a sneer, entirely humourless and obscurely menacing.

His presence came close to draining those evenings of all pleasure. But not quite. There was, for me, a kind of magic in that grimy old church hall when I entered it on training nights, feeling the usual ambiguous sense of excitement, anticipation and apprehension. The place was pungent with the mingled scents of sweat and massage liniment and loud with the sounds of thudding fists on punchball and bag, the swish and rhythmic slapping of skipping ropes, the grunts and snorts of physical effort. This, or something like it, was where those heroic figures of the ring, whose lives I had read about in the pulp magazines, had started. When the gloves were laced on and I stepped into the ring my mouth was dry with the fear of pain and humiliation, but I felt, too, a tingling eagerness for the trainer's command to begin so that I could try to put into practice some of the feints and blows that I had been secretly rehearsing during the week in the small space between the foot of the bed and the windows of the bedroom.

The club membership was divided into the junior and senior sections, each with its own trainer. I, at the age of twelve was, of course, a junior but Kenneth, who was tall and quite solidly built, sparred in the senior ring under the instruction of a paid trainer called Jack Nee. Jack was in the Royal Air Force, stationed at Halton, and he had been a good-class professional featherweight and was still young and active enough to box with his pupils of all weights and sizes and he often administered painful lessons to those of his charges who had become over-confident and were showing signs of arrogance or a tendency to ignore his instructions and employ unorthodox tactics of their own devising.

The junior trainer was a man in early middle age named Harold, and he performed his duties on a voluntary basis. To say that he did the job as a labour of love would not be too wide of the mark and, if that sounds at all cryptic, it should become clear later. He had, I believe, boxed as an amateur but not, I suspect, with much distinction. However, he knew enough to teach us young tyros the basic moves of the game, how to deliver a straight left and connect cleanly with the knuckle part of the glove, how to deflect the same blow from an opponent and how to move inside the swing or hook with short straight punches. He did not look in the least like a boxer. He wore horn-rimmed spectacles, was small and dapper with dark curly hair, just beginning to turn grey, and, when dressed to go out, he always wore a bowler hat. The Old Man, who displayed an admiration that was very close to a boy's hero-worship for Jack Nee, took little notice of Harold, who obviously did not conform to his notions of what a boxing instructor should be.

Harold owned a bicycle shop in which he sold new and second-hand machines and accessories, and performed cycle repairs. This shop was in Wendover, a small town about five miles away from Aylesbury, at the foot of the Chilterns. He lived with his old mother, whom I never met, in a flat above the shop. In a back room downstairs he had installed a floor-to-ceiling punchball and he encouraged those of his young boxers who lived near enough to visit his shop and make use of this apparatus. I was keen to be one of his visitors and to use the punchball and, it appeared, Harold was just as keen that I should. But I did not possess a bicycle and I could not afford the bus fare, so it seemed that I would have to forgo the pleasure and physical benefit of attending his little training sessions at the back of his shop until, in the spring of 1934, at the end of the boxing season, Harold mentioned that he had in stock a secondhand Hercules bicycle which had been returned because of its buyer's failure to keep up the hire-purchase payments and he would be happy to sell it to me for the bargain price of thirty shillings. This sum, though indeed very small for a bicycle that was in excellent condition was, I told Harold, beyond any realistic hope of attainment. He said, "I'll have a word with your Dad."

The Old Man's photographic business must have been prospering still more because he had recently bought his first motor car, an ancient Singer which looked like a Brownie box-camera on wheels, but I knew that he would not fork out thirty shillings for a bicycle for me. As things turned out I was wrong. Harold must have been persuasive and, evidently, the Old Man decided that cycling over to Wendover and back and working out on a punchball was much better for me than sneaking off to my bedroom with a book. Not that his decision to buy the Hercules was a very generous act. After long discussion with my mother and many days of uncertainty he finally reached the conclusion that he would pay for the bicycle, but I would have to pay the price back from my weekly pocket money of sixpence. Half of this sum was to be deducted for a period of two years and four months, after which the thirty shillings would have been returned. I was overjoyed and would gladly have agreed to receive no pocket money at all in order to be the owner of a shining, good-as-new Hercules. So one evening, after the Old Man had closed the shop, he drove me over to Harold's, the money changed hands and the bicycle was presented to me and I rode it back to Aylesbury in a state of such pure happiness that even my chronic fear and hatred of my father was subsumed or transcended. As for Harold, he was my fairy godfather. He was kind and gentle and generous, and I loved him.

At the age of twelve I was, by the standards of today and even, I suspect, by those of over half a century ago, extraordinarily ignorant. This was partly the consequence of the kind of education dished out by the elementary schools of the time and, perhaps more significantly, of the utter intellectual and imaginative barrenness of life at home. With poorly trained and underpaid teachers, large classes and inadequate facilities, the most the schools could hope to do was to produce children to be sent out into the world of work at the age of thirteen or fourteen, who could be called competently literate and numerate. Although the curriculum included history, geography and science, the way in which these subjects were taught bore no relation to the contemporary world that we inhabited and most of the teachers seemed positively to discourage what curiosity their pupils might display. At home neither the Old Man nor my mother ever, to my recollection, showed the least interest in or knowledge of politics or the arts. The only times I recall the Old Man reading a newspaper were when he was trying to find out the result of some sporting event or, on Sundays, to read in one of the cheap popular papers some item of scandal, which would be kept from us children.

I could have recited the names of every national and international boxing champion at every weight and could have supplied fairly detailed biographies of all the great fighters of the past from Bob Fitzsimmons, who won the world heavyweight title from Gentleman Jim Corbett in 1897, to my current hero, the Brown Bomber, Joe Louis, but I could not have named the Prime Minister of the day or his political party. When, in 1935 I saw at the cinema newsreels showing the destruction of the Abyssinian warriors by the tanks and dive-bombers of Mussolini it was with little interest and less comprehension, and a few months later when Hitler's troops invaded the Rhineland no minatory sound of war drums reached my ears. The scandal of King Edward VIII's relationship with Mrs Wallis Simpson did, in a vague and prurient form, filter through to the most politically ignorant of us and was discussed in a grinning, furtive way in the playground of Queen's Park School. One of our number, a fat and generally unprepossessing boy called "Dump" Rickard, seemed to possess a knowledge of the adult world of sexual intrigue that was denied to the rest of us and I recall his saying with a leer, "'Course he's going to marry her. He's got to. Everybody knows that. He's got her in the puddin' club so he ain't got no choice."

On reflection this announcement seemed to be, in all likelihood, a true explanation of the King's determination to marry the American divorcee. We all knew that if a bloke got a girl in the family way he had to marry her and not even kings could flout this inexorable law. I do believe, at this stage in my life, I was even more ignorant than most of my peers. I had only the vaguest idea of how, in fact, a man did get a girl in the family way. The onset of puberty had begun with alarming, exciting, bewildering physical manifestations. My first erections occurred at curiously inappropriate moments and caused me great embarrassment. I was in Archie Dormer's class and that good and kind man had been marking our English compositions while we were doing our "silent reading". Suddenly he called out my name and said, "Come out. I'd like you to read this to the class. It's very good. Come on. Come and read it to us."

I felt my face burning with shame. My cock was as hard as a tent-peg.

"Come on out," Archie said. "Nothing to be shy about."

Wasn't there, indeed?

I slithered out of my desk. I had to keep one hand in my trouser-pocket to hold the damned thing down. I knew that I would have to take my exercise-book and hold it with both hands so that I could turn the page. The whole class would see my condition. My terror did not have the slightest detumescent effect; if anything it had the opposite. I had to think and act quickly and I did.

I blurted, "I feel sick sir! Gotta go!" and I rushed for the classroom door, swung it open and ran through the hall and the cloakroom and out into the playground. There I paused outside the lavatories but only for a moment. I was afraid that Archie might send someone after me to see that I was all right, or even come and see for himself, so I just kept going, heading for the school gates and out into the street and away towards the canal where I would hang around until the end of the school day, before going home.

The next morning I turned up at school feeling apprehensive and when, at playtime, Archie told me to wait behind while the rest of the class went out I thought I would be subjected to a stern inquisition about my previous day's behaviour. But he said, very mildly, "I didn't know you were so shy about reading your work out loud. I wouldn't have asked you if I'd known. You needn't have worried. All you had to do was say you'd rather not. You could have asked me to read it for you. I wouldn't have minded. All right?"

He was so kind and so mistaken that I felt tears of shame and self-hatred prickling behind my eyes.

I muttered something, keeping my head lowered, and he said, "Off you go then," and I went out into the playground where my friends were waiting to see if I had been caned or punished in some other way for dodging out of lessons and trying to fool old Archie that I was sick.

I had heard about masturbation, which was always called tossing yourself off, but although I would grin and snigger with my schoolmates when the practice was referred to, I did not actually know how it was done. I have sometimes wondered whether my almost total lack of mechanical aptitude and absence of manual dexterity were responsible for my failure to find out for myself how the trick was accomplished when none of my companions seemed to experience the least difficulty; certainly I was not desisting for moral reasons or because I was afraid. The truth is that I never did find out until I was shown exactly how to do it by an experienced practitioner. It happened like this.

Once I had my Hercules bicycle I was able to ride over to Harold's shop in Wendover every Saturday and, after school had broken up for the summer holidays, I visited him almost every day of the week. We would sit together in his back room and he would tell me about famous amateur boxers he had seen and we would suck the Mintoes of which he always kept a plentiful supply. Then he would say, "Well, time we got to work!" and he would fix the punchball from floor to ceiling and time me on his stop-watch while I belted away at the ball for three one-and-a-half minute rounds. After that we would continue chatting or he would produce a draughts-board and we would have three or four games, all of which he would win.

I was to box in the National Schoolboy Championships in the coming season so we talked a lot about other boys from the Aylesbury Club who had tried for a title and the reasons for their failure to reach the finals.

"We must keep an eye on your weight," he said. "Come on. I'll put you on the scales."

To the rear of the back room was a small office, little more than a cubby-hole, and it was there that he kept the scales. He would take me into this room and say, "Get your clothes off. All of them. We've got to see your exact weight."

So I would take off my clothes and stand on the scales and Harold would examine them very carefully, and I knew that he was concentrating hard because he was breathing quite heavily.

Once, he asked me if I had a girlfriend and I said with complete truth that I had not. I had felt strongly attracted to certain girls I saw in the girls' school playground but I could not imagine any circumstances in which I could meet them. I did not bother telling Harold this, feeling that he would probably laugh at me. Quite often he would tell me jokes, many of which I did not understand, although I never failed to laugh at their conclusion. A number of these tales ended with the formal refrain: "And little Audrey laughed and laughed." When I, like little Audrey, laughed and laughed at the climax of Harold's jokes, he would smile, and look at me with a kind of mild enquiry, and I would blush because I knew that he knew the jokes were incomprehensible to me.

Then one afternoon in the last week of the holidays he said, "I've been thinking. I couldn't help noticing you're getting quite big. I mean down there. I reckon you'll have to wear a jock-strap this season."

I had seen the seniors in the club dressing-room getting into their gear so I knew what a jock-strap was.

Harold said, "Would you like me to get you one? I can order it from Gross's. They're the firm who supply all the boxing kit. All I need is your measurements."

I said that I would be grateful if he could do that.

"Doing the measurement is a bit tricky. We can do it while you're getting weighed. I've got a tape-measure in the office."

So for the umpteenth time I went into the cubby-hole, took off my clothes and stood on the scales. Then began the weird and bewildering business of measuring me for a jock-strap.

Harold said, "I don't know whether you know this, but they'll need to have both measurements of your thing — when it's big and when it's normal."

I stared at him blankly.

"You know what I mean, don't you? I want to measure you when you've got the horn. When you're hard. You understand?"

I nodded.

"Can I help you or can you do it yourself?"

"I don't know." I was wondering if Len Harvey and Max Baer and Joe Louis had to go through this perplexing and embarrassing business when they were fitted with their jock-straps.

Harold was smiling faintly, encouraging. "You do know how to do it, don't you? You *have* tossed yourself off, haven't you?"

I was ashamed to admit my ignorance. "Well . . . sometimes."

"Look," said Harold, "like this;" and he unbuttoned his fly and held in one palm for my inspection what looked like a fat, uncooked sausage. Then encircling the end with thumb and three fingers, with his pinkie genteelly cocked like a countess taking tea, he began briskly to move his foreskin to and fro, and the livid thing began to swell and take on the aspect of an animate and perhaps dangerous creature.

He said, "Take hold of mine. Perhaps that'll help you."

I had already withdrawn my gaze from his thing. I could not look at it again, far less touch it. I felt that I had failed my trainer miserably.

I said, "I'm sorry. I can't."

At once he said, "That's all right. Maybe we'll try again some other time. Don't worry. You can get dressed now," and he turned away to restore, with some difficulty, his distended member to his trousers. I said, "Won't you be able to get me one then?"

"Get you what?" Harold looked puzzled.

"A jock-strap."

"Oh. Yes. Yes, I think they'll find one that'll fit."

He went out of the office and I got dressed and joined him in the back room.

"Have a Mintoe," he said, and we sat among the bicycle spare parts, the chains and inner tubes and handlebars, sucking our sweets and talking about the approaching amateur boxing season until it was time for me to cycle back to Aylesbury.

I reached the final of the Schoolboy Championships of Great Britain the following year and I had acquired not only the promised jock-strap but a pair of proper black kid boxing boots. I also moved from the junior to the senior ring under the tutelage of Jack Nee since I, like Kenneth, had grown tall and put on weight, and the young boxers of my own age were neither big nor skilled enough to serve as adequate sparring partners. I still felt affection for Harold, but I did not cycle over to Wendover nearly as often as I used to, and when I did turn up at his shop he was often too busy with repairs to spend a lot of time with me, and though he still supervised my three rounds on the punchball he did so without the old enthusiasm and he no longer bothered to check my weight. I assumed that he had relinquished responsibility for my fitness now that Jack was officially my trainer but I did rather miss the old intimacy, the Mintoes and the games of draughts.

Despite the Old Man's regular presence on training nights and his usual criticisms of our performance in the ring I was enjoying my boxing more than before. By this time I had boxed not only in the Divisional and National Schoolboy Championships but in competitions against other clubs, and I had met with a good deal of success. At this early stage of my boxing career I had acquired a good defence and I had learnt how to make the most of my height and long reach so that I was, at that level, difficult to hit. I won most of my bouts on points. I trained conscientiously, doing a daily work-out of exercises and going for long runs, and only occasionally and with subsequent agonies of guilt did I practise what Harold had demonstrated to me when measuring me for a jock-strap.

Kenneth had left school and was working as assistant projectionist at the Market Cinema for a wage of ten shillings a week, most of which was taken from him as a contribution towards his board and lodging. The Old Man seemed to hate him with a virulence that was more powerful than the scornful distaste he showed for me, which was tempered occasionally with a grudging approval when I had boxed better than expected and won a bout against someone who was regarded as a formidable opponent. Kenneth was a much more accomplished boxer than I was, but he was less successful in competitions because he suffered so badly from pre-fight nervous strain that by the time he entered the ring he was almost too exhausted to raise his hands. That the Old Man's treatment of him from early childhood onwards was responsible for this I have no doubt at all. I do not refer simply to the physical cruelty and the fear that he provoked but to something at least as destructive and sinister. Kenneth was the ugly one of the family.

For as far back in time as I can remember I heard the Old Man's voice, vicious with spite and hatred, telling Kenneth and me, and anyone in earshot, how ugly and clumsy and generally repulsive my brother was. There were certain phrases that the Old Man used repeatedly when addressing his sons: I was usually called "a young pup", which was almost a term of endearment compared with the expressions of odium directed at Kenneth, who was variously referred to as "ugly ape", "clumsy idiot", and "disgusting animal". One of the weightiest responsibilities of fatherhood, which can work to the advantage or terrible disadvantage of the child, is that the infant will accept as incontrovertible truth paternal judgement and assurances, and the effects of these can remain when the more mature reason should have discredited them. I heard the Old Man saying that Kenneth was an "ugly brute" so often that it became, for me, an indisputable fact. More to the point Kenneth, too, was convinced of his grotesque ugliness and, as a consequence he became, in his efforts to efface himself, pitiably inarticulate and uncomfortable in even the least threatening of social encounters.

When I was in my early teens a girl I knew said to me, "I saw your brother last night coming out of your shop. Isn't he good-looking?"

At once I said, "It couldn't have been Kenneth. You must have seen someone else." I had, in a sense, been brainwashed to believe the lie of his ugliness.

I have in my possession photographs of Kenneth taken when he was a small child and later at the age of eleven or twelve, as well as in young manhood, and by anyone's standards he would be judged a very good-looking boy and adult. As with so much of the Old Man's behaviour the motivation in this matter remains obscure. I suspect that it must have sprung from some kind of jealousy but almost certainly this was not caused by his son's supplanting him in the affections of his wife. Of course, one cannot be sure about the feelings of the partners, if that is the right word, in any marriage, but I recall no overt signs of affection between my mother and father, while I do vividly remember many scenes of violent quarrelling when the Old Man's spluttering rage would be met by his wife's cold sarcasm. Furthermore, even if he felt any love or even possessiveness towards her, he could hardly have viewed the infant Kenneth as a rival because she showed no affection for either of her sons, nor did she object to, or disagree with, his vilifications of their eldest child, or his regular physical cruelty to us two boys.

After one of their quarrels, which became more savage than usual and ended with the Old Man hitting his wife and storming out of the building, he stayed away that night, and the night that followed, and it seemed that he might have carried out at last a frequently voiced threat to get out for good. But, after four days of tranquil delight, troubled only by the fear that it was too good to last, he came back and the lights were dimmed again. Any hope that he might have been chastened and humanized by the brief separation was demolished the day after his return when he gave me a vigorous thrashing because he caught me helping myself to a couple of cheese straws from the larder. Neither Kenneth nor I had ever put up more than a purely defensive and largely ineffectual resistance to his attacks, but our resentment and hatred were now fed by the insult to our growing sense of manhood and nascent dignity, and it began to seem possible that my fantasies of vengeance might, on some not far distant day, become reality.

Life at Kingsbury Square, though chilled and darkened by the Old Man's presence, was by no means always intolerable. I was in my last term at school and Kenneth was about to find a more interesting job as a photographic assistant at the Forest Product Research Laboratories at Princes Risborough. We both continued to read voraciously and I was now trying to write poems as well as prose, after reading an old anthology of mainly Georgian verse which contained some poems that seemed to me, then, to be of great beauty and a few of which have retained something of their first power to move. This book was the Methuen *Anthology of Modern Verse*, with an introduction by Robert Lynd and a dedication to Thomas Hardy, who was still productively alive when it was first published in 1921, and although I can now see that far too many of the pieces were sentimental and inept there was fine work by such poets as Hardy himself, Edward Thomas, Wilfred Owen, Walter de la Mare, and Charlotte Mew, and I now believe it was not a bad introduction to the art of poetry.

In the front room of the flat was an old upright piano which had been brought from Beeston to Market Square and on to its present place in Kingsbury Square. This was at a time when the possession of a piano was seen as an emblem of social superiority, or what later came to be called a status-symbol, which is probably why the Old Man had kept it. My mother could play, though not particularly well, and she did so very infrequently. When Kenneth was thirteen he began to show a deep interest in and love of music, and this was encouraged by his teacher Archie Dormer. After he had left school he bought a "Pianoforte Tutor" from a music shop in Silver Street and applied himself to the task of learning how to read music and to play the piano. Without any help or encouragement he succeeded in becoming a more than competent performer on the instrument, an accomplishment which won and still retains my admiration. Being two years older and, I now realize, possessing a better brain and superior instinctive taste than I, he was a valuable guide to me, first in what to read and, later, when I had developed a strong liking for music, in what to listen to. Then, in the summer of 1936, when I was fourteen years old and not quite sure whether I wanted to be a romantic poet like Rupert Brooke, or a tough boxer with scar tissue on the eyebrows and a cauliflower ear, I discovered another interest that was at least as absorbing as poetry, music and boxing. I met my first girlfriend.

CHAPTER
THREE

Eddie MacSweeney and I were no longer the inseparable friends we had been at school but there were, for a time, intermittent and usually quite brief periods when we made attempts to revive the closeness that had once existed between us, though the intervals separating these meetings grew wider until we saw each other only rarely and by chance, and on those occasions we both felt a kind of restraint that was almost embarrassment, and we would part with hearty and patently false promises of getting together again soon. In the early summer of 1936 we were attempting what must have been one of the last renewals of the old intimacy and we had gone together to the open-air swimming pool in the Vale recreation ground. It was a warm evening and the sun was still bright on the glittering water, and the shouts and laughter of the swimmers grew fainter as we left the pool and walked through the park, past the scratch games of cricket, towards the public tennis courts. We both had our towels draped round our necks and our swimming suits were negligently swinging at our sides. Eddie's hair was still damp and spiky.

He said, "Hey, look. They look a bit of all right, don't they?"

Two girls were walking slowly a few yards in front of us. They both wore flowery summer frocks and their bare calves were smooth and brown above the little white ankle socks. I felt nervous and excited and afraid that Eddie would do, or say, something outrageous and shameful. His flat, toothy face had changed little since I had first known him, and he still wore a permanent and clownish grin.

"Come on," he said. "Let's catch 'em up."

Both of the girls had dark brown hair. I had yet to see their faces. I guessed that they were about my age, or maybe a little older, perhaps fifteen. I was glad that I was taller than Eddie, and I knew that I had often been mistaken for being two or three years older than my true age, but this knowledge did not inspire much confidence. I increased my pace a little, but made sure I trailed behind my companion.

He drew level with the girls and said, "Hello, haven't we met somewhere?"

Neither of them answered, but they did not walk any faster, nor did they tilt their heads back so that they seemed to be sniffing for a bad smell, so the signs were not altogether discouraging.

Eddie was now walking at their side. He looked over his shoulder at me and beckoned with a jerk of his head for me to join him. I did so, but was still far from confident that we would not be rebuffed. I glanced at the girls' faces and looked away quickly, but not before I had seen that one of them was much prettier than her friend.

Eddie said, "This is my mate, Vernon. He's a boxer."

Both girls took a quick look at me.

"Looks more like a spaniel," the plainer one said, and they both giggled.

"I'm not kidding," Eddie said. "He's a schoolboy champion."

This, I thought, was advocacy I could well do without. The girls giggled louder, though the pretty one flicked an amused but friendly glance at me. I tried to think of something witty and sophisticated to say but nothing suggested itself.

"Where do you work?" Eddie asked them.

"We're models," the plainer one said.

Here was my chance to dazzle them with verbal wit: "What, like Hornby trains?" I said.

No one laughed, not even disloyal Eddie. I swore to myself, and at myself, and I could feel the warmth of my blushing.

"Where do you two work?" asked the prettier one.

Eddie answered cheerfully, "The Co-op."

They both seemed to find this funny.

Then the plainer one said, "What about your mate, the Spaniel?"

Before Eddie could tell them that I was still at school I said quickly, "I'm a photographer. I work for my Dad."

The plainer girl was now looking straight at me. I did not like her expression. It was faintly amused, but I could detect, too, a hint of scepticism and, perhaps, scorn. "I know who you are," she said. "You're Vernon Bain."

I did not deny it.

Eddie said, "What they call you, then?"

The prettier girl answered, "I'm Doris." She was looking at me as she spoke and I felt my heart perform a little skip and a jump. "And she's Joyce," she added.

"Hello, Joyce," Eddie said, but received no reply.

By the time we had reached the park gates I had not spoken again but I was irrationally sure, or almost sure, that Doris was well disposed towards me. We had twice exchanged glances during the walk and each time she had smiled at me and each time I had caught my breath and felt my heart's gymnastic tricks.

Eddie said, "Which way you going?" and it was Doris who answered. "We live in King's Road. I've got to be in by eight. I promised my mum."

I noticed that her speech was not of the district: she sounded like a cockney, or at any rate a Londoner. We began to walk towards her home.

I said, "You don't come from round here, do you?"

Doris laughed. "You've got sharp ears! Not likely! I come from Peckham. Where they bash you for being handsome, as my dad used to say!"

Her father's words sounded to me like, "Where they besh you for bein' 'ensome!" and, as spoken by Doris, they had a jaunty and comic note. I wished that just she and I could be together, without Eddie and Joyce.

We crossed the canal bridge and turned right and took the first turning to the left, not into King's Road itself but into the lane which afforded entry to the back gardens of the houses in which the two girls lived. There was a fragrance in the summer air of lilac or honeysuckle and from an open window drifted the sound of dance music from a wireless or gramophone.

I was beginning to fear that Doris would disappear into one of the houses before I could ask her if I could see her again but, when I spoke, I had not the courage to put the question directly to her.

"Do you have a job?" I asked.

She nodded. "Of course. What do you think I am, a lady of leisure?"

"What do you do? Where do you work?"

"You know Brown's, the electricians on Cambridge Street? I work there. I do a bit of office work, sending out invoices and that, and I serve in the shop sometimes."

"You like it?"

"It's all right. Not bad."

Eddie was attempting a little banter with Joyce but receiving little or no encouragement.

Doris said, "Here we are. Home sweet home," and she stopped at one of the back garden gates. "See you tomorrow dinner time, Joyce."

"OK," Joyce said. "Abyssinia," and she walked away quite quickly and turned into the back garden of one of the other King's Road houses without looking behind her.

"Not very friendly, is she?" Eddie said without rancour.

Doris smiled. "She's all right. She's my best friend."

"Sooner you than me."

I was about to ask Doris if I could make a date with her when a rather hoarse female voice, of a kind that I was sure my mother would describe as "common", called, "Doris! Time you was indoors! Don't hang about there! Come in and get your supper!"

I caught a momentary glimpse of a thin, rather gypsy-like little woman on the back-door step before she disappeared into the house.

Doris said, "That's my mum. Got to go. Must love you and leave you. 'Bye." And she pushed open the gate, swung it to behind her, and trotted up the path and followed her mother into the house.

Eddie said, "Not a bad bit of stuff. You should have asked her for a date."

"I know. I was just going to." I felt a sudden panic, a fear that this wonderful chance had slipped away from me, that already she had forgotten all about my existence. The next day she would be picked up by someone older, more confident and handsome, someone with a job and money, who could take her to the pictures and to restaurants, someone smartly dressed who could dance.

"Let's go and get some chips," Eddie said.

"I can't. I haven't got any money."

"That's nothing new. Come on. I'll treat you."

That night I found it difficult to get off to sleep. I could visualize Doris's face very clearly, the bright, mischievous eyes, her brown hair that held small gleams of copper and gold, the peachy softness and bloom of her cheeks, the way in which her lips, which needed no artificial tinting, parted to show small even teeth as white as peppermints. When she smiled one dimple appeared in her right cheek. Her whole aspect shone with good health and unaffected vivacity. She had said, as she left us ". . . love you and leave you," and she had looked at me as she had spoken, not at both of us, certainly not at Eddie, but me. Of course I knew that "love you and leave you" was a popular expression often used carelessly, even jokingly, but the more I thought of the smile which had accompanied her words, the more I tried to persuade myself that she was conveying to me a serious message. It was a fragile hope, less substantial than a straw, no tougher than the most slender filament, but I held on to it tightly as eventually I drifted into sleep.

The next day, after morning school I cycled back into town and propped my bike against the kerb in Cambridge Street. I walked to and fro past Brown's the electricians, peering through the windows and doorway, trying to seem casual but growing less concerned about appearances as I failed for the fifth or sixth time to catch any sight of Doris. I knew that I was already late home for my dinner and would have to face the Old Man's rage, but I continued to patrol the pavement outside Brown's. I thought about going into the shop but could think of no pretext for doing so. After another half an hour or so I knew that I could no longer delay going home. I went back to my bike and I was bending down to put on my bicycle-clips when, astoundingly, Doris appeared at my side.

She said, "I saw you going past. I just nipped out. I've got to see Joyce at one but I'm not doing anything tonight. Can you meet me?"

I could scarcely believe that this wonderful encounter was really happening.

I managed to stammer, "When? Where? What time?"

I saw the dimple appear in her right cheek and her eyes sparkled with laughter.

She said, "Seven o'clock at the end of the lane. I'll come on my bike and we can go for a ride." Then she was gone.

I rode home. My luck still held: the Old Man was out photographing a wedding and my mother didn't bother listening to my excuses.

"Your dinner's in the oven," she said. "It'll be ruined but that's your look-out."

I don't think I could have eaten even the most splendid meal. I was feverish with excitement, anticipation and an almost incredulous rejoicing in my good fortune.

That evening Doris and I went for our cycle ride to a village called Weston Turville; there we parked our bikes and walked through fields to Halton Reservoir where a few people were swimming, and we promised ourselves that next time we came we would bring our bathing things. The thought of this was profoundly thrilling. She would take off her clothes; I would see her almost naked. I would show off my crawl like Johnny Weissmuller, the American Olympic free-style champion who had become a movie Tarzan. We held hands as we walked. She told me that her father had died when she was twelve. She still missed him very much. I found it difficult to imagine anyone missing a father, but I murmured sympathetic noises. And then we kissed. That first kiss was more symbolically significant than sensuously pleasurable, though it was not long before we became more expert and improvisatory, and found deep enjoyment in our experiments.

I think it was on our second or third date that I admitted to Doris that I was still at school but, though she was surprised and amused by my confession, it made no difference to our growing closeness, except that she cheerfully paid for most of our material indulgences such as ice-creams or sweets or visits to the cinema. At first I was ashamed and reluctant to accept her bounty though this soon passed and I told her that in a few weeks the term would end and I would leave school and get a job and be able to treat her as a proper boyfriend should. Doris was generous in every way. She gave affection, material gifts, and the most precious gift of herself, with impulsive recklessness.

When the term ended and I had left school I started to look for a job in the "Situations Vacant" columns of the local newspaper. The trouble was that I was ill-equipped for any kind of work. My manual ineptitude and impracticality disqualified me from any job that called for the simplest mechanical skills, and my having had only an elementary education and, of course, no School Certificate or any other qualification seemed to rule out work in local government or a bank or any kind of office. The Old Man tried to teach me, as he had more or less successfully taught Kenneth, to do his developing and printing, but everything I touched seemed to go wrong and after a few sessions in the dark-room I was chased out with his curses echoing in my stinging ears, which had been soundly cuffed.

Thursday was the early closing day for Aylesbury shops so both Doris and I were free in the afternoon. On one of these half-holidays in August we cycled over to Halton Reservoir and after we had been for our swim and had dried and dressed ourselves I suddenly thought that we were now quite close to Wendover and it would be nice to take Doris to meet my old friend and mentor, Harold. She was quite agreeable, as she was to most of my suggestions, so we rode off side by side along the country lanes until we came out on to the main Aylesbury road to Wendover. I was pleased to be making the visit because I had for some time felt rather guilty about my neglect of my former trainer who, I was sure, would be pleased to see us.

When we arrived at the bicycle shop we dismounted, parked our bikes, and I led the way inside. The doorbell sounded its familiar note and I heard a noise from the back room and Harold appeared blinking at us through his horn-rimmed spectacles.

"Hello," I said, "I've brought my friend Doris to meet you."

To my surprise and disappointment he did not look especially pleased to see us. He gave Doris only a quick nod of what could scarcely be called anything as friendly as a greeting, and to me he said, "I'm very busy at the moment. Got a lot of repairs to do." I was puzzled by what sounded like a note of reproach beneath the irritable impatience.

"All right," I said. "We've been for a swim at the reservoir. I just thought we'd come and see you, being so close. Never mind, if you're so busy. Come on, Doris. Let's go."

If I thought my peevish tone might bring about a change in his attitude I was mistaken.

We left and got on our bicycles and started to ride back to Aylesbury.

I said, "I don't know what was up with old Harold. I've never known him like that before. He always used to be so pleased to see me."

Doris was smiling in a rather mysterious, secretive way. "It was me he didn't like," she said. Then she added, "I think he was jealous."

"How could he be? That's silly. And I'm sure he liked you. I can't imagine anyone not liking you."

Doris still smiled to herself but said nothing and soon we began to talk about other things. What she sensed, or suspected, in her only meeting with Harold I never found out because this was the last time we ever spoke of him. As for me, in my ignorance, I had no inkling of what she might have meant and, though this now seems almost unbelievable, even to myself, I had no suspicions of Harold's unorthodox sexual preferences until, some fourteen years or so later, I was talking to an old boxing club acquaintance on one of my rare visits back to Aylesbury and Harold's name was mentioned. My companion's wife was present and it was she who said, "Oh, that old fairy. We all wondered how he managed to keep out of gaol."

For a fraction of a second disbelief made its tiny silent protest; then illumination flooded in and all became startlingly clear. Harold had indeed been my fairy godfather. And that was what Doris had been smiling at all those years ago, and smiling, too, at my ignorance, or what would probably seem to her to be my innocence. I suppose Harold could reasonably be called a child molester: I suppose, too, that I was, in a mild way, sexually abused by him when I was a boy. Odd that I was not aware of it until, in my late twenties, I heard a not especially sophisticated woman call him an "old fairy".

I have sometimes wondered why, since Harold's deviancy was suspected fairly widely, the Old Man did not get wind of it, but I am sure that he remained in complete ignorance, and the reason for this was that, like many egoists, he was blinkered by his own self-absorption to the reality of other people. In addition to this, those who did know of, or suspect, Harold's proclivities would not be likely to mention their doubts to the Old Man, because his demeanour discouraged intimacy. He was a man without friends. I think that I was about seventeen when I began to understand dimly why this was so. For one thing his peculiar snobbishness erected fences against the possibility of friendship. He regarded himself, quite irrationally, as being in some way superior to the men who came along, either as officials or as interested spectators, to the boxing club. This was something to do with owning his own business and possessing a motor car. He kept himself aloof, almost as if he were afraid of being contaminated by the "commonness" or the comparative poverty of those men who were mainly factory workers. But there was another related and probably more insurmountable barrier to his forming friendships: this was his enormous vanity which manifested itself in simple physical narcissism — I have seen him spend long periods in front of a mirror, lost in a self-admiration that seemed to verge on adoration — but

71

this was only the outward sign of a deeper, metaphysical vanity and self-love that precluded the need for close companionship.

When I was very young, between the ages roughly of six and nine, the Old Man would tell me stories of his boyhood and of his exploits as a soldier in the First World War. In all of these tales he played a heroic role. At first I accepted them as a true chronicle of his exciting younger life but, as the same tales were repeated, always with embellishments and sometimes with quite startling increases in the importance and reckless courage of his part in events, I began to wonder about their historical veracity, until his boasting became something of a secret joke between Kenneth and me. In all of the pre-war boyhood stories the Old Man featured with a boon companion, Alf Chadwick, who was a kind of page or squire to the Old Man's gallant knight. Alf was a vague, colourless figure who loyally accompanied his gifted and courageous leader in exploits of derring-do; he held the Old Man's coat while the bully was soundly thrashed; he was rescued by his resourceful chum from what would have been certain death by drowning in the Manchester Ship Canal; he stolidly blocked the bowling while, at the other end, the Old Man scored his century. And so on.

In 1935, when I was thirteen, the whole family had made a trip to Eccles where my maternal grandmother, with whom I had lived for a blissful year when I was eight, still occupied the tiny two-up-and-two-down terrace house in Bardsley Street. While we were there Kenneth and I were taken to the Belle Vue fairground in Manchester by our uncles and treated with tolerant and generous good humour. Then, on the day before our planned return to Aylesbury the Old Man said that he was going to call on his old pal, Alf Chadwick. We were all bundled into the car and off we drove into one of the Manchester suburbs. All I remember of the place was that it was one of those dull thirties housing estates with rows and clusters of identical little red brick houses with tidy identical gardens. We drew up outside one of these and were told to get out of the car. Then we trailed after the Old Man as he pushed open the little gate and walked up the path to the front door and rang the bell. After a pause the door opened, but not fully, and a thin, medium-built, clerkish-looking man in a knitted pullover, grey flannels and carpet slippers peered out.

The Old Man said, "Hello Alf. Remember me? Jim Bain?"

The man did not open the door any wider. He stared, unsmiling, at his visitor. He did not seem to notice us. This was the legendary Alf Chadwick, Sancho Panza to the Old Man's youthful Don Quixote.

"Long time since we met, eh Alf?"

Alf Chadwick still stared wordlessly at the Old Man and I thought I could see a look of something close to horror in his eyes. Then his lips moved. I did not hear what he said. Whatever it was, it could not have been more than a couple of words. Then, without saying anything further he firmly shut the door.

We turned round and went back to the car and clambered inside. The Old Man started the engine.

I spoke to the back of his head. "What did he say?"

There was a pause before he answered. "It was inconvenient. He said it was inconvenient."

We drove away. Kenneth and I, who were sitting in the back of the car with Sylvia between us, exchanged grins, but we both admitted later that, for the first and only time in our lives, we had felt sorry for him.

Doris and I saw each other almost daily through the summer of 1936 and, when the autumnal evenings brought the early darkness and a faint premonitory chill, we went for walks, seeking places of solitude for tremulous and, on my part at least, clumsy love-making. Under the star-entangled branches of an oak tree in Turn Furlong Lane Doris bared the twin moons of her breasts for me to nuzzle and kiss. Our busy lips and hands aroused a passion that alarmed as much as it thrilled me. We did not then, or ever, perform the ultimate penetrative act itself, though I think this restraint was due to my fears rather than to any caution shown by Doris. The new boxing season had just begun and the superstitious conviction that sexual indulgence was fatally debilitating, firmly held by everyone in the game, was a nagging cause of anxiety. I was afraid, too, of Doris becoming pregnant, and the nightmarish prospect of announcing the unhappy event to the Old Man made me sick with fear. He had quite often, in his rages with Kenneth and me, used the melodramatic words, "I'll swing for you!" and we had come to regard the threat as something of a joke, but now I seriously thought that he would be capable of killing me if I were to tell him that he was to become a grandfather.

If the initiative had been left entirely to Doris I believe that we would have consummated our avowed love. She showed none of the apprehension that so troubled me, for she was braver, more loving and generous than ever I could be. Her passionate frankness and joyful response to whatever erotic overtures I made were undervalued by me. I do not mean that I lost, in that prim phrase, my "respect" for her. But I do believe that her honest enjoyment of the sensual pleasure she derived from our love-play, her complete lack of coquetry and dissimulation did tend to reduce for me, if not eliminate, that sense of female mystery which is part of the male erotic experience. We used the words of love to each other, those tarnished, banal little verbal trinkets, the phraseology of popular song and movies and pulp magazines — "I love you darling", "I adore you", "I am yours for ever", and in the first weeks after our meeting we exchanged love letters, even though we were seeing each other four or five times a week. But, for me, it was not long before the momentous trivialities of the lovers' world became commonplace; even our love-making began to lose its piercing, dizzying sweetness. She was still my girl and one day, we told each other, we would be married. But I was beginning to notice other girls, their difference, their mysteriousness, their secrecy. I cannot say with certainty that I loved Doris. I think I did. I hope I did; though, even if I'm right in thinking so, I'm sure I did not love her as she deserved to be loved. The odd thing is that I can truthfully say that I do love her now.

CHAPTER
FOUR

It was early in 1937, not long after my fifteenth birthday, that I succeeded in finding a job. I answered an advertisement in *The Bucks Herald*, which asked for the services of a junior clerk, preferably with matriculation, to work in the offices of a firm of Incorporated Accountants. I wrote, in my most careful handwriting, a letter of application in which I made no reference to my having attended an elementary school; I admitted that I had not matriculated, but said that I hoped to rectify this and would be studying at evening classes. To save the cost of a stamp I delivered the letter by hand to the offices, which were near to the National Provincial Bank on the High Street. I had to tell the Old Man about my application because he would not have supplied notepaper and envelope unless I could provide a good reason for needing them. He asked to see the advertisement and I showed it to him.

He said, "You don't stand a chance. Didn't you read the thing? See what it says? Matriculation. That means they want a grammar school boy. You're wasting your time."

"It only says 'preferably'," I pointed out. "They might not get anyone with matric applying."

He scoffed at my optimism but, rather surprisingly, he handed over the stationery.

A few days later I received a letter asking me to attend for an interview. The firm of accountants was based in Oxford and it had a couple of branches in Buckinghamshire and Berkshire. I was interviewed by Mr Baker, one of the partners, who came over to Aylesbury once or twice a week to see important clients. In his absence a Mr Harris acted as manager and he was assisted by a younger man of about twenty-six called Albert and a married typist named Laura.

Mr Baker interviewed me in his rather dingy office on the second floor. He was small with short and frizzy grey hair, and bright clear eyes, birdlike behind gold-rimmed spectacles. His accent was decidedly posh and he spoke very quickly as if impatient to get the interview over and apply himself to more serious matters. I was to discover much later that this brusque manner of speech was habitual and was symptomatic of extreme shyness.

He said, "Are you good at maths?"

"Yes," I lied.

"What do you do in your spare time? Hobbies, sport, that sort of thing?"

I was not expecting this. "I read a lot. And I box."

"What did you say?"

"I said I read a lot."

"No, the other thing."

"I box. I belong to the Aylesbury Boxing Club."

"Really? I see."

I could not tell whether he regarded boxing as a desirable activity or not.

"Accountancy is mainly common sense really," he said.

I nodded and sat before him trying to look sensible.

Then he added, as if speaking to himself, "Trouble is, common sense is a rather uncommon human attribute."

I nodded again.

There was a pause while he shuffled through some papers on his desk. I saw that my letter was among them.

Then he said briskly, "You would start at fifteen shillings a week. The hours are nine to six. Thursday would be your half day. At first your duties would be mainly filing and answering the telephone. As you learnt more the work would become more interesting. We'll let you know if and when we wish you to start. Have you any questions?"

I had no questions.

As I was leaving he said, "You'll hear in the next day or two."

A couple of days later word arrived telling me that I had been given the post of junior clerk and that I should start work at nine o'clock on the following Monday.

The Old Man sniffed and his mouth went down at each corner in the familiar deprecating smirk. "Accountant! You can't add up two and two. You won't last very long there. You wait and see."

But he was wrong. As Mr Baker had said, accountancy, or the very simple aspects of it with which I had to deal, was mainly common sense. It was also pretty tedious.

My first job on arrival in the morning was to file away in their appropriate folders the carbon copies of the previous day's outgoing mail. I shared the office on the ground floor with Laura, the typist. She was a woman in her thirties, tall and thin but quite good-looking in a way that seemed to belong to a slightly earlier period. This impression might have been caused by her absence of obvious breasts, a certain gaucheness of carriage, and her pale hair which was worn quite short in a sleek, cap-like bob. Not that she was lacking in femininity. She always exuded a quite heady scent and she wore flowery dresses and glittering jewellery — earrings, bracelets and rings. I soon realized that Albert, who had a small office of his own on the first floor, was in love with her in a hopeless and doggy way and that she encouraged his devotion in a manner that was both flirtatious yet motherly, and not very different from her treatment of me. I was a little in love with her myself in an even more hopeless though perhaps less doggy way than Albert.

I had my own desk in the ground-floor office. In front of me was a small and ancient switchboard on which I could transfer outside calls to the other offices or simply use it as an intercom. After I had done the filing I would sit at my desk and check the accuracy of long lists of figures given to me by either Albert or Mr Harris. This process was called checking the "casts" — adding up was always called "casting". Quite quickly I became expert in casting lengthy columns of pounds, shillings and pence at great speed and with almost infallible accuracy, an acquired ability which caused me some surprise at the time and, perhaps more strangely, one which I have retained into my present advanced age.

It was not long before I was given tasks of a little more complexity, checking ledger entries with invoices and bank statements and working out a kind of equation, details of which I have long since forgotten, called a bank reconciliation. I was also responsible for petty cash and the "post book" in which the recipients' names and addresses of all outgoing mail were recorded along with the cost of the stamps used on the envelopes. After only a few weeks I found that I could practise some small-scale embezzlement without much fear of discovery so I was able to supplement my wage with weekly sums of a shilling or so. I had recently finished what had seemed the interminable paying off of the cost of my bicycle; I was allowed to keep only four of my weekly fifteen shillings so, even with the sums of which I was defrauding my employers, I was still a lot less affluent than Doris, whose mother made no deductions from her wages.

Both Albert and Mr Harris were pipe-smokers. I liked the smell of their tobacco and the whole business of filling and lighting their briars seemed to me a pleasing and adult activity, one that I grew increasingly covetous of. So one Saturday lunch time I went into Woolworth's and bought a sixpenny pipe, and from there I visited a tobacconist where I purchased an ounce of Tom Long mixture and a box of Swan matches. On Saturday afternoons I was in sole charge of the Baker premises because that was when the rest of the staff took their weekly half-day's holiday and I was free to read and write and practise on Laura's typewriter. So, alone in the office, safe from possible mockery or disapproval, I filled the pipe and, with a good deal of difficulty and wastage of matches, I managed to get it lighted. I puffed away, trying to convince myself that I was enjoying the hot, acrid smoke that filled my mouth, filtered down into my lungs and gradually created a small bluish fog in the room. After a few minutes of this I began to feel dizzy and vaguely ill, and then I felt a clenched fist of pain in my stomach that grew larger and weightier. I just managed to reach the lavatory on the first-floor landing before I was horribly sick.

Strangely, this experience did not deter me for all time from smoking. On the advice of Albert, who had seen my Woolworth pipe lying on my desk and expressed dismay that I should have tried to smoke it, I later bought for two shillings and sixpence a "reject" from a recommended tobacconist on the High Street. "Reject" meant, Albert explained, that the pipes so labelled had been deemed by the famous manufacturers — because of some tiny flaw imperceptible to any but the most expert eye — unfit for sale. In fact the small imperfections were usually irregularities in the grain of the wooden bowl and this only affected slightly the appearance of the pipes, not their function. Albert also advised me to choose a mild Virginia tobacco, at least to begin with, and, although many weeks passed before I began to find any enjoyment in smoking, I persevered, though never of course, at home.

Since I was working a forty-eight-hour week, with only Sunday completely free, training at the boxing club on Wednesday nights and attending evening classes on Monday and Tuesday, it seemed that I would not have much time for meetings with Doris. She, however, found what was at least a partial solution to this problem by enrolling for the classes I was taking in bookkeeping and commerce. These evening lessons were held in Queen's Park School and I found it an odd sensation to go back to my old school, accompanied by my girlfriend, and sit with her in the classroom where Eddie and I had, not so very long ago, spent countless hours of boredom, mischief, daydreaming, and had even done a little work. I found the bookkeeping classes moderately interesting and I had little difficulty in grasping the principles of double-entry, trial balances, profit-and-loss accounts, and balance sheets. The "commerce" lessons, which were concerned with simple economics and office organization were, I found, dull and of no relevance to my job so Doris and I played truant from these and spent those evenings either in the cinema or, if there was no film worth seeing, we would find a secluded place to exchange kisses and caresses and promises of eternal fidelity and love.

My relations with the Old Man at this time took the form of a wary avoidance of anything approaching either intimacy or contention. It was not difficult to keep out of his way now that I was going out to work and he was busier than ever in his photographic business. He must have been doing well, for it was at this time that he was able to get rid of the old Singer and buy a brand-new Hillman Minx. I boxed in the Junior ABA Divisional championships and was beaten in the final when my opponent, a boy from Barnet called Lewis, accidentally opened a fairly severe cut over my left eye when his head struck mine and the referee had to stop the contest. The Old Man was disappointed but his disappointment did not manifest itself in the bitter rage and recrimination that any failure of mine or Kenneth's usually provoked. I think he regarded a defeat of this kind as an honourable one, and he could console himself, as he did, with the probably deluded belief that I would have won except for the accidental cut. Then the precarious peace that had existed between us for weeks was suddenly disrupted.

Doris and I had been to watch a film at the Pavilion Cinema on one of the evenings on which I was supposed to be at my commerce evening class. We had come out at about half-past nine and I had walked home with her and we had spent perhaps half an hour in the lane behind King's Road before our final goodnight kiss and my heading for Kingsbury Square. It was well after half-past ten when I arrived. Everyone except the Old Man had gone to bed. He was waiting in the living-room wearing his executioner's expression. This was quite different from the more usual half-smirk that somehow combined derision and self-regard. His lips were pressed firmly together in a straight line and his eyes bulged with a barely suppressed rage and incredulity.

He said, "And where have you been?"

"Evening class."

"Look at the clock."

I did so.

"Well?"

"We hung about a bit after we'd come out. Went and had some chips."

"And who is 'we'?"

I guessed then that he was in possession of some incriminating knowledge.

"A couple of chaps who go to the same class."

"What's their names?"

"Cooper and Hardy." Gary Cooper had been in the film that Doris and I had seen. Hardy might have been suggested by Thomas Hardy, whose poetry I had recently been reading or, perhaps more likely, by the Andy Hardy movies starring Mickey Rooney, which were popular at that time. "Tom Cooper and Jack Hardy."

"You're lying," the Old Man said, injecting a charge of venom into the second word.

I did not answer. I felt myself blushing and I knew that I looked guilty. He was not yet ready to produce whatever proof he had of my mendacity. He was standing in front of the fireplace.

"Come here."

I stayed where I was, just inside the room.

"I've got to go to bed," I said.

"You'll stay where you are!" He moved a couple of steps closer to me. "You've been lying, haven't you?"

I made a little grunting noise in my throat which could have been either denial or affirmation. I was preparing to cover up against the attack which I knew would be coming.

"I can't hear you," he said. "Answer me so I can hear. You've been telling me lies, haven't you?"

I nodded. "Yes."

"All right. What have you been doing?"

"I went to the pictures."

"Who with?"

"A friend."

"And what's your friend's name?"

I considered for half a second inventing another name but as quickly discarded the idea.

I said, "Doris."

"What? I can't hear you. Speak up!"

"Doris!" It was almost a shout and carried, I think, a note of defiance.

"Doris," he echoed, with a twist of his mouth as if the word tasted unpleasant. "You went to the pictures with Doris, did you? And who might Doris be?"

"Just a girl."

"Just a girl. Hasn't she got a second name?"

"I don't know."

He swung with an open-handed right and I ducked instinctively so that the slap landed high on my head, but the quickly following back-hander, travelling upwards, caught me on the tip of the nose, and the sharp pain brought moisture to my eyes.

"Don't you look at me like that, my lad!" he said. He was breathing heavily, probably more from excitement than physical exertion. "Tell me what this Doris's second name is."

"I've only just met her. I didn't ask her."

"You're lying! You've been seen with her before tonight."

I said, "She's just a friend."

"A friend, is she? A friend that gets you to skip your evening class to go to the pictures. And what were you up to after the pictures? You came out at a quarter-past nine. Don't argue because I know. You were seen. What about the next hour or more? What were the pair of you up to then?"

"I took her home."

"You took her home, did you? And where's home? Where does she live?"

"King's Road."

"Whereabouts? What number?"

"I don't know. I left her at the end of the road. I didn't see what number."

"So you left her at the bottom of the road. You must have got there by nine-thirty at the latest. To get back here'd take you twenty minutes at the outside. So what were you and this Doris doing for three-quarters of an hour at least? Tell me that."

"Talking."

"You were talking, were you? For three-quarters of an hour you stood out there in the cold just talking. What about? What did you find so much to talk about?"

"We talked about the picture. And other things."

"I bet you did! Now listen to me. I know you think you're a big man. Going out with girls. Wasting your time when you should have been studying. You think you know it all. Well, let me tell you you know nothing! You're just a conceited young pup. You're too young to go out with girls. Plenty of time for that when you're grown up. Keep your mind on healthy things, on your work, your training and boxing. More young boxers have been ruined by girls than by anything else. You understand?"

I nodded.

"I said, do you understand?"

"Yes."

"You don't want to end up like your brother, do you?"

This sudden introduction of Kenneth into his diatribe puzzled me.

"You hear what I said? You don't want to be like your brother, do you?"

All I wanted to do was get away from the Old Man to my bedroom. I shook my head and mumbled a noise that could be taken as negative, but my lack of understanding must have shown.

"You know why he's like he is, don't you?"

I waited, wondering what he was raving about.

"Why do you think he's so disgusting? Why does he lose his fights? Why is he so feeble? He does things. To himself. Filthy things. You understand what I'm talking about?"

I nodded.

"Do you understand?"

"Yes." And I suddenly did.

"I hope you don't do those things."

"No."

"I will know if you do. It shows. You know I'll be able to tell. So promise me you won't."

I made another noise that was meant to be affirmative. I thought that I wasn't really lying either. I rarely had need to do filthy things to myself when I had Doris who was happy to do them for me.

He said, in what was meant to be a conciliatory voice, "I know you've got more sense than him. So stick to your training. You could win a Junior ABA title next season. And don't mess about with girls."

I said, "Can I go to bed now?"

"When you've given me your word."

"All right."

"You won't see this girl any more?"

"No."

"Go on. Clear off then."

I went up the stairs to the bedroom which Kenneth and I shared. I thought he was asleep but when I climbed in by his side, being careful not to awaken him, he said, "Been having a nice little chat?"

We spoke in low voices in case we should be heard. "Warnings about girls. The terrible harm they can do you." I did not say anything about the Old Man's vilification of Kenneth. He'd heard it all from the donkey's mouth anyway.

"Is he going to swing for you?"

"Not tonight. Nearly, but not quite."

"Silly bugger."

I turned on my side and settled down for sleep.

Kenneth said, "I'm going to get a new record on Saturday."

"What is it?"

"A woman called Marian Anderson. She's singing 'Softly Awakes My Heart' from *Samson and Delilah*. She's a black woman, terrific voice. Contralto."

"Good," I said and we both soon fell asleep.

Kenneth and I had managed between us to save enough money to buy a gramophone pick-up. This was an electric turntable which could be plugged into an ordinary radio and the sound was relayed through the wireless's speaker. Slowly we were managing to accumulate a collection of records. Kenneth, who earned more than I did, contributed more, financially, to the buying of these records and, even if this had not been the case, I would still have left their choice to him. During the next year or so we had acquired, apart from the Marian Anderson record, Debussy's *La Mer* and *Prélude à l'après-midi d'un faune*, Paderewski playing Liszt's "La Campanella", Gigli singing arias from *La Bohème* and *Turandot*, Lawrence Tibbett singing the "Largo al Factotum" from *The Barber of Seville*, Schubert's Unfinished Symphony, Beethoven's *Egmont Overture*, and other vocal and instrumental works. Kenneth's playing of the piano improved wonderfully, and music became an increasingly important source of consolation and delight, though our enthusiasm for literature did not diminish.

We were both reading, among other things, much prose and poetry dealing with the First World War. Neither my interest nor Kenneth's in this tragic and mythopoeic event was caused by an awareness of the imminence of another global war, for we were both quite ignorant of what was happening in Nazi Germany or in the rest of the world. My interest in, or what might almost be called obsession with, the Great War of 1914–1918 began in very early childhood. I suspect that most, or many, people of my generation — those who were born during or shortly after that war — are haunted by its imagery, its pathos, the waste, the heroism and futility. We were brought up with the echoes of the artillery barrages, the iron stammer of machine-guns, the cries of the wounded, the songs and martial music, sounding in our ears. There seemed to be pictures of no man's land, of the trenches, the shattered landscape, barbed wire, ruined farms and churches, everywhere we looked.

I remember when I was no more than six or seven years of age collecting photographs with glued backs so that they could be easily stuck into a flimsy little album which, like the pictures, was given away by one of the twopenny weeklies for boys. One of these photographs showed tommies in steel helmets, greatcoats, and puttees, grasping rifles with fixed bayonets, clambering over the parapet of a sandbagged trench behind an officer who held a revolver; another showed a tank ploughing through the mud and debris of a battlefield, and yet another showed dead German soldiers sprawling in a gun-emplacement. There were many more, and they all seemed to merge in the mind into a composite picture of corpses and guns and cratered desolation. The same images and forlorn landscape had appeared on the flickering screen at the Beeston Picture Palace: the films — of which all I now remember are the dug-outs, trenches and the vast dark blooms of explosions as the soldiers fell against the barbed wire or into muddy craters — might have supplied the military vocabulary of Flanders that I seem always to have known of, Very lights, whizzbangs, Jack Johnsons, trench-mortars, Lewis-guns and howitzers. Since those were the days of "silent" films there were no sound-tracks to convey appropriate music, though a solitary pianist sat in darkness below the screen to play "mood music", so it might have been from that source that my familiarity with the popular songs of the war came: the marching tunes, "Pack up Your Troubles", "Tipperary", "Take me Back to Blighty", and those yearning laments for a paradisal peace that had gone for ever, "A Long Long Trail", "Keep the Home Fires Burning" and "If you were the Only Girl in the World".

The Old Man had served in the Great War. He claimed to have joined the army when he was fourteen and to have been wounded at Mons. These claims may have been true, and I have sometimes wondered if the experience of modern warfare at such an early age, and his subsequent marriage to a frigid and misanthropic woman, could have been responsible for turning him into the man and father he became. But I have never been completely convinced and, while he was willing and even eager when I was small to tell implausible stories of his own bravery and resourcefulness in the trenches, it was noticeable that he showed no interest in the books dealing with the war that Kenneth and I brought home.

It was at this time in Aylesbury that we discovered the County Non-Fiction Library in Pebble Lane, which was a spacious and well-stocked repository of specialized academic books, including poetry, literary criticism and biography. The chief function of this establishment was to supply books of a serious kind to the branch libraries throughout Buckinghamshire if they were specially requested by readers, but Kenneth and I somehow learnt that we could withdraw books directly, and we took full advantage of this. It was from there that we borrowed Siegfried Sassoon's *Memoirs of an Infantry Officer* and Edmund Blunden's *Undertones of War*, both of which we enjoyed, but it was Robert Graves's *Goodbye to All That* which I found the most captivating. It seemed to possess a freshness, vigour and directness that the more mannered prose of Blunden and Sassoon did not offer. In these books and in the poetry of Owen and Sassoon I found myself entering the world of terror and bleak beauty that had haunted my early childhood and I experienced a sense of recognition, as if, in an earlier incarnation, I had myself fought and suffered on the Western Front.

Of course we were not reading only poetry and autobiography. A year or so earlier Penguin Books had brought out their first paperbacks at sixpence a copy and, among the titles issued, was Hemingway's *A Farewell to Arms*. Kenneth was still friendly with a boy who had been at school with him and who was now an apprentice at Hazel, Watson & Viney, the printers of those early Penguins, and this boy was able to smuggle out free copies for us. Both Kenneth and I were overwhelmed by Hemingway's novel and I mistakenly thought that his style, the simple sentences, the deliberate repetitions of words and cadences, would be easy to imitate, and I began my own Great War novel, which shuffled painfully along for a few exercise-book pages and then collapsed never to rise again. I also read, around this time, Forster's *Howard's End* and, on Kenneth's recommendation, Fielding's *Tom Jones*, both with great enjoyment, so it seems that I, with my brother's guidance, was beginning to show some signs of literary discernment, though it is true that we were reading, probably with equal pleasure, novels by such lesser authors as Hugh Walpole, John Galsworthy and Richard Aldington.

My reading of poetry was less wide-ranging than Kenneth's but, in a sense, less conventional, perhaps, for a boy's early exploration of the art. Of course his two years' seniority and intellectual maturity accounted for some of this difference of taste but it was, I believe, more to do with the ways in which each responded to poetry. Kenneth was reading not only the romantics Keats, Shelley, and Wordsworth, but Milton and Pope, while I chose to read and re-read mainly poetry of the late nineteenth and early twentieth centuries. Although I enjoyed Masefield's narrative poems, *Dauber* and *Reynard the Fox* and Arnold's *The Scholar Gipsy*, my preference was for short lyrical descriptive verse and I was living proof of T. S. Eliot's assertion that poetry can communicate before it is understood, for I would have found it very difficult to say what many of the poems, which I genuinely enjoyed, were actually about. I do not mean that I simply listened to the sonority of the language without bothering about what the words were telling me. I doubt if anyone could respond to any kind of literature in this way. But it did seem that the conscious, analytical part of my response was often lulled into a kind of stupor by the rhythms and the richness of the imagery of the poetry I was reading. I had not yet arrived at the point where I would understand that the pleasures of poetry could be far more various and invigorating than the languors that I was then content to experience, that the proper reading of a poem was not an act of passive submission but one of collaboration with its author.

The poems that I was myself trying to write were attempts to imitate the melancholy cadences and misty images of the kind of verse I enjoyed and I am sure they were all comically inept. The only one that I now recall in any detail was entitled "The Day that Summer Died" which began:

> From everywhere the mourners came
> The day that Summer died,
> From shores of sleep and dreamland,
> From vale and mountainside.

Then the next three stanzas gave a whimsical account of who the mourners were, personifications of the constituents of the English autumnal scene, leading to the conclusion:

> The trees all stood in silent grief,
> The wind lay down and cried;
> And Beauty came in sombre robes
> The day that Summer died.

I was very proud of this poem and when I showed it to Kenneth and he was only mildly approving I tried to hide my disappointment. Doris thought it was lovely but, then, she said the same thing about every poem of mine I showed her, some of which even I had come to recognize were pretty feeble. In spite of Kenneth's less than rapturous reception of "The Day that Summer Died"

I was so sure of its merits that I showed it to Laura at the office and she, too, thought it was lovely. So 1938 saw my sixteenth birthday and, later in the year, the Munich crisis and, much more important to me, the conviction — based upon foundations the extreme flimsiness of which was mercifully concealed from me — that I was one day going to be a poet.

CHAPTER
FIVE

All I now remember of the Munich crisis of September 1938 is a feeling of mild excitement followed by a sense of equally mild anti-climax. If I had even heard of the Sudetenland, which is unlikely, I would not have been able to point to its location on a map or globe. If there were a threat of war, naturally it would come from the Germans, for they were "the enemy", the Boche, the Hun, the Kraut. Neville Chamberlain had promised us that there would be peace in our time and he ought to know. I was much more concerned with two momentous discoveries: D. H. Lawrence and beer. My liking for the second of these proved more durable than that for the first, but to begin with I found swigs of the prose of *Sons and Lovers* and the stories collected in *The Prussian Officer* and *The Woman Who Rode Away* more intoxicating than the bottled brown ale with which Kenneth and I began our drinking careers before graduating to the stronger and more palatable draught bitter that became and remained for a long time our staple drink.

The introduction to Lawrence came about through reading John Middleton Murry's *Son of Woman, the Story of D. H. Lawrence* which I had found in the Pebble Lane library. The more I read of Lawrence's work and that of his exegetists the more excited I became, and the fact that my understanding of what I was reading was far from complete served only to increase the excitement. Here was a great writer, a poet, a prophet, a sage, who seemed to be saying that true wisdom was not to be found through the exercise of reason but that it resided in the senses, in the blood, in the guts, and was to be attained through a surrender to the deepest and darkest of our bodily desires. Great stuff and especially attractive to a youth of undeveloped cognitive powers. I did not notice, or at any rate consciously notice, the cruelty, arrogance and deep misanthropy that ran through almost everything Lawrence has written, though, when I came to read the poems, I was less impressed by those about animals, and I could not fail to hear the note of almost hysterical anger in the curious poem, "Bibbles", nor to be puzzled and shocked by his readiness, at the end of "Mountain Lion", to swap "a million or two of humans and never miss them" for "that slim yellow mountain lion".

I was still reading quite a lot of Georgian verse, much of it of the hearty open-road kind, and Kenneth and I often spent our Sundays walking on the Chiltern Hills above Wendover. Somewhere, perhaps in Eddie Marsh's *Memoir of Rupert Brooke*, we had read that the young poet had walked on these same hills and had found an inn called the Leather Bottle where he had lunched on beer and bread and cheese. Certainly we knew Brooke's poem, "The Chilterns" and were fond of reciting:

Thank God, that's done! and I'll take the road,
    Quit of my youth and you,

>The Roman road to Wendover
>By Tring and Lilley Hoo,
>As a free man may do.

On one of our walks we succeeded in finding the Leather Bottle, a small ale-house that was also a farm, and we were able to buy beer and bread and cheese as Brooke had done just over a couple of decades earlier.

I developed a taste for beer much more quickly than I had learnt to enjoy smoking a pipe, though, at first, as with the pipe, it was the idea and its associations rather than the taste which tempted me to adopt the habit. To begin with I found even the sweetish and mild brown ale quite bitter to the palate, but once I had grown accustomed to this new flavour, so different from the sugary and effervescent mineral waters I had been fond of, I quickly came to enjoy both the taste and the effect of slight euphoria that it induced, and was soon demanding something a little stronger in the form of draught bitter. With my pipe and my tankard of ale I felt I might easily be taken for a real poet like one of those I had seen in book illustrations — someone like Lascelles Abercrombie or Wilfrid Gibson. But this was my Sunday self, and only in summer and early autumn. In the weekday office, with my analyses of sales and bought ledgers and bank reconciliations, or being sent down to the baker's shop to fetch cakes for our four o'clock tea, it was impossible to sustain this delusion, and when the boxing season started in October the poetic pipe was put away and I became, or aspired to become, the broad-shouldered, slightly flashy and swaggering hard case, the fighting man.

The bond of love between Doris and me had been slowly weakening for some time. Her kisses had long since lost much of their power to thrill and our embraces had become almost perfunctory; even the brightness of her eyes and warmth of her smile had been dimmed by familiarity. The mystery, the whispered secrets of women's sexuality, the dangerous but thrilling ferity beneath the soft and floral daintiness, were possessed by strangers, girls seen on the streets, riding past on the upper decks of buses, smiling to themselves, dreamy with their private knowledge. I knew all about Doris, or thought I did. Our separation occurred almost without my noticing it. By the spring of 1939 we had ceased to meet and when I saw her walking down the High Street with someone I did not know, a young man clearly older than myself, the sense of dispossession and jealousy was not strong enough to hurt very much and even curiosity was too mild to be troublesome and it quickly evaporated.

Perhaps our intimacy would have continued if it had been based on some common interests other than the simple enjoyment of each other's kisses and caresses, but the fact was that I could not share with her any of my excitement about literature and music, neither of which held the least attraction for her. At first I had tried to ignore her lack of interest and understanding and had subjected the poor girl to long and incoherent discourses on whatever novels or poems happened to be my current enthusiasm. She was too generous and affectionate to let her boredom show in any obvious way but too honest to dissemble convincingly.

After we had parted I did, at times, experience

moments of regret and would sometimes rehearse in my mind scenes of reconciliation, but these were scarcely any more realistic than the other fantasies I wove, all of which were variations on the single theme of an encounter with an ideal girl in whose person were combined great beauty, intelligence, a taste for music and poetry and, of course, passionate devotion to myself. Details of her appearance remained both vague and variable, though there was a period, just after I had seen the film of *The Barretts of Wimpole Street,* when her features appeared more clearly and they bore a marked resemblance to the actress who played the part of Elizabeth Barrett Browning, Norma Shearer. I did not know at the time that Elizabeth had been forty years of age when she eloped with Browning and had not looked much like a romantic actress.

The heart was not satisfied for long on a diet of fantasy, and it grew not so much brutal as hungry for more substantial fare. Then in the early summer of 1939 I saw a living girl who might prove to be an incarnation of the ideal of my dreams if only I could make her acquaintance. My first sight of her occurred one lunch time when I was on my way home from the office. She came out of Brook House, a large building at the entrance to Kingsbury Square which contained the offices of the Inland Revenue, firms of architects and solicitors and, though I did not know this at the time, the premises of a ladies' hairdressers. She was walking just in front of me and she wore a light summer dress and high-heeled shoes and her legs were slim and beautifully shaped. Brown curls were clustered at the tender nape and she walked briskly, her heels tapping on the pavement like little castanets. I had to overtake her to see if her face would fulfil the promise of what I had so far seen and I had to do this without making the manoeuvre too obvious. I walked past her swiftly as if on an errand of some urgency and as soon as I had put about a dozen yards between us I stopped abruptly, pretending that my attention had been caught by something in the window of a shoe shop. Then, as she drew almost level, I risked what I hoped would appear to be a casual glance at her face. I was not disappointed.

She did not look in the least like Norma Shearer. In fact she did not seem to me then, nor did she ever seem, to be "beautiful". That was not the word for the instant and intense attractiveness of her face, which from that moment became for me the prototype, not of feminine beauty, but of desirability. It was the kind of face you never see on a big woman, small delicate features with something piquant, a hint of the *gamine* about their very slight irregularity, the tiny tilt of the small retroussé nose, the almost imperceptible projection of the upper front teeth, the mouth small but full-lipped like a tempting confection, a delicious jujube. Her eyes were dark brown and looked faintly amused and very self-possessed. I thought it was the most exciting, provocative, lovely face I had ever seen and I felt dizzy with longing for her.

I thought she must be, like me, taking her lunch hour so I went home for my meal and then returned to the street to hang about, waiting for her return. She did not appear. I waited for as long as I could then went back to work. That was the beginning of my being haunted

101

by her. In the following weeks I saw her many times but always for tantalizingly brief periods and once, to my distress, she was with a tall, well-dressed and horribly good-looking man who must have been at least in his late twenties. I guessed that she was quite a lot older than I was but, somehow, I was able to go on hoping against all reason that one day she would be my girl. One lunch time I followed her to where she lived, a Victorian terrace house on the Buckingham Road, and I spent many summer evenings patrolling the area for a glimpse of her leaving or arriving at the house but I saw her only once, when she was carrying a suitcase and making for the bus depot in Kingsbury Square. I followed her like a private eye and saw her catch a bus to Buckingham, but I knew that the route it took wound through many villages at any one of which she might alight so I had learnt nothing new about her. Sooner or later I would have to find the courage to approach her and ask her to go to the pictures with me. And at last I did.

It was an August evening and I was taking the office mail to the post office, my final task of the day. I shoved my stack of envelopes into the letter-box and turned away and found myself face to face with her. The shock was like a blow under the heart. I gasped, and then, incredibly, I found that I was speaking.

"Hallo," was all I said.

She smiled but did not reply. I watched her post her letter and when she turned to walk back up the High Street I walked with her.

I said, "I've seen you around a lot."

This time she did answer: "Yes. I've seen you, too."

I glanced sideways at her and she was smiling faintly and I knew that she must have been aware of my frequent shadowing of her over the past weeks and months.

"There's a good film on at the Odeon this week," I said.

"Is there?" Her voice was quite low in pitch but level, almost toneless. She sounded bored.

"*Pygmalion*. It's a play by Bernard Shaw. Leslie Howard's in it. It's supposed to be very good."

When she received this information in silence I was seized suddenly by a kind of panic of self-consciousness and I could think of nothing further to say. Perhaps she was struggling to conceal her laughter that a young office junior, now earning twenty-five shillings a week, of which he was permitted to keep only six, should have the impertinence to accost her. The walk at her side was beginning to take on the quality of a dream and not an entirely pleasant one. We reached the top of the High Street with Kingsbury Square on the right and Market Square on the left.

I gestured to the left. "I've got to go this way."

She stopped walking and turned to face me. That faint suggestion of a smile on her lips and in her eyes was still there. This was the first time I had really had the chance to look at her in close-up, face to face. The moment outside the post office had been too unexpected and too brief. Now I just stared at her as if my eyes were tasting the sweetness and astringency that were somehow mingled in the conjunction of eyes and lips and in that smile that might have been mocking me.

With something close to desperation I said, "You wouldn't like to go and see it? With me? *Pygmalion*, I mean."

"When?" She now looked impassive, completely calm, detached.

I could scarcely believe that she seemed to have accepted the invitation.

"Tomorrow?"

"I can't tomorrow. Thursday would be all right."

A great flower, a rose perhaps, seemed to be spreading its scent and its petals in my breast; catherine-wheels and sparklers were whizzing and glittering in my skull. "What time? Where shall we meet?"

She named the time, seven o'clock, and the place, outside the cinema.

"I'll see you then," I said, and I turned and walked blindly away across the Market Square. After a few paces I stopped and turned to look back at her but she had disappeared. My pure elation was suddenly darkened by a stain of fear and anxiety: something terrible might prevent her from coming; she might have been agreeing to meet me simply to get rid of me; she might encounter a man, rich and handsome and mature and fall in love with him and forget all about me; she might, even now, be run over or about to fall mortally ill. Thursday was a great distance away. The time would pass very slowly. Then I realized that I still did not even know her name.

My anxiety did not disappear but it changed its focus and became less fanciful, concerning itself with more immediate and practical matters. The first of these was money. Thursday was the day before I was paid and already I had spent my current week's pocket-money. Second, and related to the first, was the question of my age or, rather, my youth. I was almost six feet in height and was generally assumed to be a good deal older than my true age. I had never, for instance, been refused a drink by a landlord or barman since I had started visiting pubs at the age of sixteen. My lovely anonymous girl would think, like most people who did not know, that I was at least twenty-one and earning a salary commensurate with that age. Taking her to the cinema in the most expensive balcony seats and buying her chocolates or ice-cream, if not both, would cost me a whole week's pocket-money. At least. So, first, I had to persuade my mother to advance me my weekly allowance; I knew any request to the Old Man would be fruitless and, in any case, would involve close interrogation as to why I needed the money.

I succeeded in getting the advance from my mother by telling her that I needed it for a textbook on accountancy which Mr Baker had recommended that I should study. I would depend on her lack of interest in any of my activities for her to forget to query its failure to materialize. Kenneth was able to lend me a shilling and I "borrowed" three from the office petty cash which would either be repaid or, as was more likely, concealed by faking the post-book. So I set out to the Odeon on Thursday evening with ten shillings in my pocket, my mouth dry and pulses racing with excited anticipation. I arrived at the meeting place ten minutes early and by the time seven o'clock struck I felt that I had already been waiting a long time. The next ten minutes seemed even longer, and still I waited and still she did not come. At twenty past seven mere impatience had been replaced by misery, anger and humiliation. She was not going to come and she had never had the least intention of turning up. She had probably forgotten all about me by now, or maybe she was laughing at the thought of my growing unhappiness as I stood without hope outside the cinema. Then she was there, suddenly, at my side, saying in her flat, inexpressive voice, "Have you been waiting long?"

Anger did not at once dissipate and I was inclined to sulk. I thought of Doris who was rarely, if ever, late and how apologetic she would have been if she had kept me waiting for a fraction of the long vigil I had been subjected to.

I said, "What happened? Did you forget we had a date?"

"No, of course not. I was a bit late getting back from work and it took me longer than I thought it would to get ready."

I detected no contrition in her voice. That she looked enticingly lovely did not mitigate the feeling that I had been badly treated. It seemed as if, by making her unattainable, her self-assured attractiveness was holding me at a distance, and I felt clumsy and unprepossessing. We walked into the cinema foyer and passed the confectionery counter on our way to the pay box. I did not, as I had planned, offer to buy chocolates. I bought two balcony tickets, which cost me four shillings and sixpence, and we climbed the heavily carpeted stairs and were led by the torch-bearing usherette to our seats. A newsreel was being shown, some Indian soldiers disembarking from a troopship at Suez, followed by boring scenes of French and British politicians shaking hands with Russians in Moscow. Then the main film started.

The cinemas of my youth always seemed to me to possess a glamour, a veiled promise of something more than what was ostensibly being offered. There was the scented darkness, the great opulent folds and drapes of the satin curtains that concealed the screen before the show began, the seductive music from theatre organ or amplified gramophone records, the soft velvet-covered seats, so close together; the collective sense of expectancy. Usually my attention was completely absorbed once the film was under way but on this occasion, sitting close to this girl, this woman, whose name I still did not know, I could not follow the events on the screen. Every few moments I glanced at her profile in the silvery blue twilight from the screen as she looked, calmly attentive, at the film. I thought about holding her hand but it would have been like taking the hand of a complete stranger, someone who might cry out in fear and outrage. I felt cheated, still angry, resentful, ashamed. I might as well not have been there for all the sign she gave of being aware of my presence. After a while I tried to concentrate on *Pygmalion* but it was impossible. Her proximity was too distracting. I could not prevent myself from flicking furtive glances at her composed and tranquil features and never once did she seem conscious of anything except the events being enacted on the screen. The evening that I had looked forward to with such anticipation was turning out to be an ordeal, yet it was one which I did not wish to end. But end it did.

The lights came up, the national anthem was played, and we joined the crowd trailing out into the summer night and began to walk towards Buckingham Road.

"Did you enjoy it?" I asked.

"Yes. It was very nice."

We walked a bit further. Then I said, "What's your name?"

"Sally Herbert." A few seconds later she added, "What's yours?"

I told her.

"Meg used to know a boy called Vernon."

"Who's Meg?"

"My sister." She said this as if I should have known.

I restrained myself from saying, "Of course. How silly of me to ask." Instead I asked her where she worked.

"Yvonne's."

"Where?"

"Yvonne's."

"Is that your sister too?"

She laughed. "No, silly. It's a hairdresser's in Brook House."

"That's the place where the Inland Revenue has offices, isn't it? I didn't know there was a hairdresser's there."

She didn't seem to consider this needed a reply.

We reached the Royal Bucks Hospital and turned right,

108

down Buckingham Road. It was a clear, mild night, the sky a quite pale shade of blue, and the stars sprinkled over it looked no bigger than sugar-grains.

I said, "I saw you getting on a Buckingham bus one day. You had a case."

Evidently this needed no answer either.

"Is that where you come from? Buckingham or somewhere on the way."

"Yes."

"What, Buckingham itself?"

"Yes."

"So you're in digs here?"

"Yes," she said, "and here's where they are."

We had reached the front gate of the house I had once followed her to. She stood with her back to the iron gate and smiled. "Thank you for a nice evening."

I wondered whether she expected me to kiss her but she did not give me a lot of time to decide one way or the other. She said, "Goodnight, then," and turned and opened the gate and walked up the short path of the front garden to the door. I watched her open her handbag and find the key and let herself into the house. She did not look back at me as she closed the door.

I walked slowly home trying to recall something worth treasuring among the evening's disappointments but the only small consolation I could find was in the reflection that I had not spent more than the price of the cinema tickets and, after I had paid Kenneth back his shilling, I would still have four and sixpence left for the weekend's pub crawl. The feeling that I had stupidly mishandled the events of the evening and had lost forever the chance of something magical nagged at me persistently. Sally Herbert had been a disappointment. And yet she still retained the power to enchant. I felt that it was somehow my fault that she had seemed dull to the point of inanity. I wished that I could go back to the time before I had ever spoken to her, the time when she was a distant embodiment of erotic fancy, infinitely desirable, remote and untouchable as a ghost yet instinct with the warmth of bodily passion, ideal but human. I did not think she would ever want to speak to me again. Nothing, I was sure, could erase from her mind the version of me she had carried away with her tonight, clumsy, gauche, sulky and immature. I would not be given another chance.

CHAPTER
SIX

By the time war was declared on 3 September 1939, even Kenneth and I must have known that it was not unexpected though I doubt if we had much idea of its causes beyond a vague understanding that Hitler had invaded Poland and that Britain and France were not going to let him get away with it. We knew, of course, that conscription had been introduced a few months earlier for young men aged twenty and twenty-one and that, during the past year, precautions had been taken all over the country against the effects of bombing and poison gas.

Two days before Neville Chamberlain's announcement of war thousands of children had been evacuated from London and other so-called "vulnerable areas", and some of these refugees had been sent to Aylesbury which was considered an unlikely target for enemy air attacks. Until the outbreak of war the Old Man, who never looked much further than the headlines of the *Daily Express* or the *Sunday Graphic*, had repeatedly announced that there would be no war, that the Germans were bluffing and Hitler had bitten off more than he could chew. Far from being depressed by his predictions proving false, he viewed the imminent conflict with relish. It would be good for business, he exclaimed. With general mobilization and conscription everyone would want their photographs taken, wives and sweethearts for their menfolk to carry with them, and the servicemen, proud in their new uniforms, as mementoes for those they left behind. Income tax would be increased, he said, but he had ways of dealing with that.

I had heard him speaking to Mam about this before and I had gathered that a fairly large percentage of cash receipts was not recorded in the account books nor put into the bank but stashed away in some secret place. I had sometimes thought that it might be nice to know the whereabouts of that hiding place but I was sure he would not risk leaving his illicit savings where I might be likely to find them. His meanness had not lessened with increasing prosperity, though he was quite generous to himself, and that year he had exchanged his car for a superior model. Sylvia, who was now twelve years old, was attending a small independent school for girls in Aylesbury but he had not been persuaded to part with the money for fees without long and acrimonious arguments with Mam, who had finally won by pointing out that his own social standing would be raised and that ultimately this was good for business.

I still saw Sally from time to time in the streets of Aylesbury and she always smiled and said hello but not with sufficient warmth to encourage me to ask her to go out with me again. Each time we passed one another on the same, or opposite, sides of the road I felt that the possibility, if it had ever existed, of our becoming intimate had receded a little further. Her attraction for me had not diminished at all. When I saw her I was pierced and shaken as if by a small electric charge that also brought with it a fragrance and taste that was delicious yet indefinable. Even when I visualized her, as I did so often, it was always with a flutter of excitement and longing and a catching of the breath. The fiasco of our one evening out together and the absence of sparkle or even mild interest in the few things she had said seemed now to have been a reflection of my own dreariness. Then one Saturday evening as Kenneth and I were on our way to the Bull's Head I saw her in a small red car driven by a sporty-looking young man with dark curly hair. They were both smiling and seemed to be in animated conversation as the car drew away from the traffic lights and gathered speed and disappeared past the Bell Hotel at the other end of Market Square.

That evening, over our Younger's Scotch Ale, Kenneth and I talked less about the books we were then reading than about what rôles we were going to play in the drama of the Second World War, and my sight of Sally being driven away by her putative lover strengthened my resolve to enlist very soon, preferably in some particularly hazardous branch of the armed forces. Already friends of ours had gone into one or other of His Majesty's Services. Eddie MacSweeney, who had been in the Territorials, had been mobilized and was training "somewhere in England". Ivan, the "sissy" son of "Uncle" Bob Linacre, whom the Old Man had pummelled so shamefully in our front room at Chilwell Road in Beeston, was in the RAF and would soon be shot down and killed with the rest of his bomber crew over Germany. Freddy Hansen, a Queen's Park boy whom Kenneth and I had often hidden from because, though amiable enough, he bored and embarrassed us with his earnestness and lack of wit, was training as an air gunner. He, too, was killed early in the war, as were George Farmborough, a friend of Kenneth's, who became a pilot, and "Chicken" Cheney, another school friend of mine, who lost his life at Narvik in Norway. But these sadly premature deaths were yet to come and Kenneth and I were armed with the confidence of youthful optimism and depthless ignorance. It seemed to us then that it was just a matter of our choosing which uniform to wear in which to seek and find adventure and acclaim.

Life at the office was becoming almost intolerably dull and I spent more time surreptitiously writing poems and stories than doing the work for which I was being paid. On Saturday afternoons, when I had the premises to myself, I did not even pretend to be about my employer's business but quite openly read whatever author was my passion of the moment, or filled sheets of the firm's paper with unfocused, febrile prose or attempts in *vers libre* at expressing the bitter disillusionment of a man who had seen too much of the world's betrayals and cruel jests. Something like that. I had discovered the Moderns, Pound and Eliot and, in prose, Joyce and Woolf. *The Waste Land* presented fewer problems to me than it would have done to a more intelligent and cultivated reader because I was still absorbing poetry through the senses, with very little co-operation from reason, so that I found it, apart from the lines in foreign languages and a few of the proper names, no more "difficult" than, say, Browning's "Fra Lippo Lippi" and a good deal more accessible than "Sordello". I was especially fond of Eliot's "Preludes" and "Rhapsody on a Windy Night" and thought I might manage something in the style of those but, though I tried often and hard enough, my attempts never seemed to look or sound much like their models.

The boxing season started again and, though I no longer trained with the old fanatical dedication, I went along to training nights, now a fully fledged senior and taking part in "special contests". These were the three or four bouts of either four or six rounds which were the main attractions, details of which were shown on the posters advertising the tournaments. The larger part of the evening's sport was taken up with three-round contests between members of the host and visiting boxing clubs, but the "special contests" usually featured holders of amateur titles of one kind or another and only rarely did a local boxer take part in one of these. The value of the prizes awarded to special contestants was considerably higher than of those given to the team boxers, so both my greed and vanity were satisfied by my being elected to take part in a special contest at Aylesbury Town Hall in a tournament to be held at the end of January. My opponent was an RAF champion called Teakle. I had seen him fight and I knew that he was a good boxer with an unnervingly hard punch in either hand so I was by no means confident of my ability to beat him. On the other hand I could give myself some reassurance by reflecting that I had been defeated only three times in my career and had recently scored a comfortable points win over a former National Schoolboy Champion called Lovell who was well-known for the power of his punching. I was not going to worry too much, at least until Christmas was over, when I would cut out smoking and drinking and get down to serious training.

The annual office party was held on the evening before Christmas Eve, our last work day before the short holiday. This function was organized and conducted on a very small scale. There was nothing official about it; in other words Mr Baker took no part in it and may well have been ignorant of its occurrence. What happened was this: the three senior employees, Mr Harris, Albert and Laura, clubbed together to buy a couple of bottles of sweet British port-style wine and some sausage rolls and mince pies. A clerk and a typist from the estate agents who had an office in the same building were to join us and they would bring a bottle of similar cheap booze and some dainty paste sandwiches which the typist had prepared at home during her lunch hour.

At six o'clock in the evening, typewriter-covers were placed over the machines, I posted what little mail there was to be dispatched, and Laura and I went up to Mr Harris's room where he and Albert were fixing up paper-chains and tinsel which had seen much service and would, no doubt, see much more. The couple from the estate agents, Derek and Peggy, came in a few minutes later bearing the sandwiches and wine. Paper hats were handed round and a half a dozen balloons were inflated and disposed about the room. Mr Harris produced a packet of Wills' cheroots and the men, including me, lit up. Laura had brought glasses from home and these were soon filled and raised in toasts and the contents were swallowed. Peggy, who had a thin pointed nose and wide amazed eyes, was soon overcome by giggles. A sprig of mistletoe had been hung on the lintel of the open door to Albert's office and Derek and Mr Harris began their annual campaign of persuasion to coax Albert and Laura to enact the appropriate ritual beneath this. We all knew it would happen, but not yet.

The room became misty with cigar smoke. I got rid of my half-finished cheroot and ate a sausage roll. Mr Harris's tie had slipped a little beneath its starched collar and he wore, with his paper hat, a rather wild grin. His eyes looked different; they had a strange glitter. He was encouraging everyone to drink deeply of the port-style wine which was very sweet and slightly viscous. One of the balloons was released from its moorings and swatted round the room until Mr Harris applied the burning tip of his cheroot to it and laughed delightedly at its explosion. The time was approaching when the kissing had to start.

"Come on!" Mr Harris cried. "Let's see you young 'uns under the mistletoe! Wish I was young and single. I'd be there a bit sharpish!"

Albert who was already quite rubicund from the effects of the wine and the warmth of the room blushed a deeper shade and grinned and looked strangely furtive. Derek from the estate agents said, "All right, Peggy? How about it, then?"

Peggy lowered her head and giggled but put up no resistance when Derek took her by the waist and drew her to the open door and gave her a quick and not-very-well-aimed kiss at the corner of her mouth. There was a muted cheer from the rest of us and Derek came away from Peggy and held out his glass for Mr Harris to refill it as if he had earned a reward.

"What about you, young fella-me-lad?" Mr Harris said, his unaccustomed joviality having a curious freezing effect so that I could feel the party grin on my face becoming stiff, a petrified rictus of embarrassment.

Laura said, "Come on, Vernon. Christmas comes but once a year," and she led me by the hand to the mistletoe where I felt her thin, unyielding body lightly touch mine and her dry lips brushing my own. I knew that this was the signal for Albert to make his move.

I left Laura standing in the doorway and she called, "Albert! Your turn! You can't get out of it. Come on!"

I watched him go towards her, his eyes alight with expectancy, the awkward smile like a grimace, his blush burning more furiously, and I knew that this was the moment for which he had been longing, this single kiss, brief and public, which would have to last him for another twelve months. Their kiss did last a little longer than Derek's with Peggy and mine with Laura, and it might have given some sensual pleasure to the principals. For Albert's sake I hoped it had, though I could not imagine those dry unfleshy lips offering much satisfaction and I thought of my right hand resting low on Laura's back as we performed our small parody of osculation and the feel of some tough, unwelcoming undergarment that would have surely discouraged sexual desire.

We dutifully applauded their kiss. The last of the wine

was poured and, a little later, Laura's husband arrived to take her home and the Christmas party came to an end. It was by then about eight o'clock. Outside, the pavements were black and greasy with the cold mist. There were quite a few people about but they were only dark shapes in the lampless streets. The few cars and buses on the High Street nosed their way along cautiously, their headlamps hooded with only the narrow slits permitted by the wartime regulations for slender and feeble beams of light to filter through. I felt restless and the few glasses of nasty but quite potent wine that I had drunk at the party had left a dry and rather unpleasant sweetness in my mouth. What I needed was a cool refreshing beer.

I had reached the turning to Kingsbury Square, on the corner of which stood Brook House, though it was totally blacked out so that not even the outline of the roof was visible against the heavy starless sky. I stopped to decide whether I should continue into the Square and have my drink at the Red Lion or turn left and cross over to the Bull's Head. I heard a sudden noise behind me and looked round quickly to see the door to Brook House swing open, and for a second I could see, silhouetted in the dim light of the vestibule, the quite unmistakable form of Sally Herbert, and then the door swung shut as she stepped out into the darkness.

I said, "Sally!" It was probably the alcohol that I had swallowed which gave me confidence. "It's me. Vernon. Can you see?"

I could only just discern the pale blur of her face as her retreating footsteps stopped and she turned towards me. I moved close and reached out and touched her arm. The faint fragrance of her scent sweetened the night.

"Come and have a drink," I said.

There was only a very slight pause before she answered: "Where?"

"Over there. The Bull's Head. I was just on my way."

"All right."

My hand was still on her arm. I kept it there and steered her to the pavement edge and together we crossed the road and made our cautious way to the Bull's Head saloon bar. There were a lot of people there and the air was thick with tobacco smoke and the noise of conviviality but I spotted a couple of unoccupied chairs at a small table under the blacked-out window and I ushered Sally towards them and, when she had sat down, asked her what she would like to drink. On each of the few occasions that I had previously been with a girl to a pub — a couple of times with Doris and once with someone called Kate, the sister of an old school friend, whom I'd tried briefly and without conviction to make Elizabeth to my Browning — I had found my partner to be ill at ease and hopelessly indecisive about choosing what to drink. Sally seemed perfectly comfortable in the crowded bar and she asked without a second's reflection for a half of bitter. Not only her decisiveness but her choice pleased me greatly, mainly because of the relative cheapness of the drink, but also because she seemed to be displaying an unexpected originality. I had believed that women always drank stuff from delicate little glasses, cocktails, gin and orange or lime, sherry, that sort of thing. The notion of the small and rather dainty Sally with a tankard of bitter was oddly titillating.

I came back from the bar with our drinks and sat down facing her. She was wearing a fawn camel-hair coat against the winter night chill. I asked her if she would like to take it off but she shook her head and raised her tankard and said, "Cheers!"

We both drank. I was still feeling inexplicably confident, yet more than this: there seemed to be something pre-ordained about our meeting, as if all my past longings and dreams were now to be fulfilled, as inevitably they had to be.

I said, "Funny seeing you like that. So late I'd have thought you'd have left work ages ago."

"I was doing overtime. Late appointment. We get very busy at Christmas."

"I'd just been to the office party."

She took another drink of her beer. "Was it nice?"

"Terrible. Old Harris, the manager, getting a bit tight. A couple of glasses is enough. Chap I work with called Albert getting all excited over kissing the typist under the mistletoe. Sad really."

"I bet you kissed her."

I shook my head. "Not on your life." Then I said, "I'll be glad to get away from Baker's. Won't be long now."

"Are you being called up?"

This was a bit tricky. I could not possibly let her know that I was well under the age for conscription but I doubted if she would believe that I was much older than twenty-one.

"I'm volunteering," I said. "RAF."

"That's what Bertie's doing. He's going to be a pilot."

I felt a stab of jealousy. "Good old Bertie," I said.

"He's my brother."

The stab-wound healed instantly. I couldn't prevent myself from beaming happily. "Is he older than you?"

"No, he's only twenty three."

My God, I thought, she's over twenty-three! What would she say if she knew she was drinking with someone who wouldn't be eighteen until the following month?

I finished my beer. "Would you like another?" I said. I had calculated in my first visit to the bar that I had enough cash for just one more round.

"Please." She emptied her tankard and I went away to obtain refills.

When I had returned to our table I said, "I saw you a week or two ago in a car with some chap. A little sports car. You were driving down Market Square towards Walton Street."

"That would've been Bertie."

"Your brother? Has he got a red sports car?"

"Yes. It's an Austin Ridley."

I felt an upsurge of relief and joy. "I thought it was — you know — chap you were going out with. Boyfriend or something."

She laughed.

"Have you got one? A boyfriend?"

"No one special," she said.

Her laughter now lingered as a little smile. Those very slightly prominent upper front teeth looked as white as

122

the flesh of a coconut against the bright red of her lips. Kissing her would be something altogether different from the brief encounter with Laura's unvoluptuous mouth.

I said, "Do you go home for Christmas?"

"Yes. Bertie's picking me up after work tomorrow."

"Lucky Bertie. Wish it was me."

"That's what you say."

"It's true."

Thoughtlessly I drained my tankard then remembered that I had exactly fourpence-halfpenny in my pocket. Sally was already finishing her drink and obviously she would expect another. The only thing to do was to pretend I had lost my wallet. I started to feel in my inside jacket pocket and then began to pat at my person like a Hollywood cop frisking a suspected hoodlum.

Sally was opening her handbag. "I'll get the next," she said.

I continued searching my pockets for a moment and then I said, "It looks as if you'd have to anyway. I seem to have left my wallet somewhere."

She was opening her purse. "Here," she said, extending a ten-shilling note, "Use this. You can owe me the change."

We each had two more beers and it was almost ten o'clock when we left the Bull's Head and started off towards Sally's digs in Buckingham Road. After the brightness of the bar it was impenetrably dark, and very cold. I held her hand and led her slowly along until gradually our eyes grew accustomed to the night and we were able to walk with a little more speed and confidence. The four beers on top of the wine I had drunk at the party had reinforced that early sense of self-assurance and I chattered easily as we walked.

When we reached the gate of the house where she lived she did not, as she had done after our dismal visit to the cinema, offer a little speech of thanks for the evening's entertainment and head briskly for the front door. She kept her hand in mine as we stopped and faced each other. I could just make out the small glitter of her eyes in the darkness.

I said, "I want to see you again."

"Yes."

"Soon."

"Do you really?"

I put my arms round her. I could smell the scent of her hair. "You know I do. I think you are the loveliest girl I've ever seen. I've always thought so, the very first moment I saw you."

I kissed her forehead and then her lips. I pulled her very close and her mouth was fresh and soft and sweet on mine. Between kisses I babbled words of love and endearment. I don't know to what extent I was intoxicated from the wine and beer; I suppose I must have been, a little; but I was certainly drunk with erotic excitement and ineffable gratitude for what was happening. Yet still, a strange conviction of the inevitability of it all persisted.

I said, "You're mine. You must be. I love you. You must always be mine."

Sally's responses to all this were not so rhapsodic as my own wild protestations but they were sufficient. She did not draw away from me. Her kisses became more passionate and more and more unrestrained. I felt that if our heavy winter garments had not been restricting our embraces she would not have resisted, would even have welcomed, a closer, deeper exploration of each other than circumstances allowed. And as we kissed and murmured and nuzzled, the image of Sally in the bar, and walking along the street, was vivid at the edge of consciousness, and I found the contrast between her neatness and tranquillity, the appearance of cool self-containment that she always displayed, and this present warm and abandoned girl who moaned softly in my arms thrillingly provocative.

We must have stayed at her gate for almost an hour before she said, "I've got to go in now."

"I don't want to leave you."

"I don't want to go but I've got to. I've lots of things to do. I've not packed for going away tomorrow and Bertie's picking me up from work."

"When shall I see you again?"

"After Christmas."

"When? How soon? When do you come back?"

"The day after Boxing Day. I start work again on Tuesday."

"So do I. Can I see you on Monday?"

"In the evening, yes. I expect Bertie'll bring me back in the afternoon. I ought to be able to get out by about seven."

We agreed to meet at the top of Buckingham Road and, after one last long kiss, Sally went into the house.

I started back towards home. I had never before felt so buoyantly, so soaringly, singingly, happy; never so triumphant and grateful, so proud and humble and fearful.

125

I could still taste her kisses, and her scent was still in my nostrils or in my head. I said her name aloud, not too often, just every twenty paces or so. I didn't think its delicious taste would ever lose its flavour but I didn't wish to feed on it too gluttonously. "Sally," I said, and felt the word melt on my tongue and be swallowed and become a part of me.

CHAPTER
SEVEN

I was about to go to meet Sally when the Old Man, who was listening to the Weston Brothers on the radio, called me back as I was leaving the room.

I stood at the open door. "Yes?"

"Where are you going?"

"I'm going to meet someone."

"Who?"

"Alan Wilde." This was the name of a friend, or perhaps I should say a former friend or acquaintance, for I had not seen him more than a couple of times during the past three months.

"And what are you going to do?"

"I don't know. Maybe go to the pictures."

"You should be going for a run. Get some road work done. This fellow Teakle is a good 'un. You'd better be fit or you'll be in for a hiding."

"I'll be fit."

"Without doing any training, I suppose. That's you all over. You think you're a big man, don't you? Oh no, you don't need to train like other boxers. You can just get into the ring and take anybody on and lick 'em. Well, let me tell you, you're going to get a shock this time unless you buck up your ideas and get down to it."

He was looking at me with his peculiar glare, eyes wide and protuberant. Something of my dislike and revulsion must have shown in my expression for he added: "And take that look off your face or I'll wipe it off!"

I was then almost eighteen years old, a couple of inches taller than his five feet nine or ten, and he had long ago abandoned the practice of sparring with Kenneth and me once he had realized he could no longer hit us at will and was in danger of being thumped himself. I was sure that I could deal with any attack from him, if I were able to contend with it as though facing an opponent in the ring or an assault from a stranger. What I was less certain about was whether I would be able to treat him like this. As a young boy I had composed vengeful fantasies of beating him up once I was big and strong enough. I had not understood that my fear of him would not entirely disappear as I grew up, that it had rooted itself too deeply in the soil of infancy to be easily eradicated, and although Kenneth and I could now despise and even ridicule him, the fear, no less potent because strongly tinged with disgust, was still present, irrational, almost superstitious.

"I'll go for a run after work tomorrow," I said. "I know how good Teakle is. I've seen him fight. I'll get fit all right."

"You'd better."

I nodded agreement and made a move to close the door behind me but he spoke again: "And another thing."

I paused, waiting.

"You and Kenneth were seen in the Bull's Head. I expect you both think you're very clever. Big men.

Drinking beer. I suppose you think that's the way to get fit." He obviously expected an answer.

"We only had half a pint."

"You shouldn't be in one of those places at all. You're under age, anyway. There's nothing clever about it, drinking beer. Nothing manly."

"No."

"Then why do you do it?"

I said, "I've got to go. I'll be late."

"Never mind about being late. Does Alan Wilde drink? Go into public houses?"

"I don't know. No. I don't think so." I was beginning to panic. Sally would be waiting in the cold night unless I could get away at once.

"You spend too much time at the pictures, slopping around, reading books. It's not healthy."

I nodded.

"You should get into the fresh air. Chop some trees down."

Kenneth, either fortuitously or by design, came to my rescue. He said, "Can I switch the wireless off? I'd like to practise for a bit."

"No, you can't!" the Old Man snapped. "I'm listening to it."

I seized my chance to slip away. Once outside, despite the black-out, I began to run. I took a short cut along Pebble Lane and through a couple of side streets which would bring me out quite close to the Royal Bucks Hospital and Buckingham Road. On my way I crashed heavily into a lamp post but I reached our meeting place just as Sally was walking towards it.

My arriving breathless seemed to amuse her.

"It's not funny," I protested. "I ran into a lamp post and nearly knocked myself out. I was afraid I'd be late and you wouldn't wait for me."

She neither confirmed nor allayed the fear, but said, "Where shall we go?"

I had forgotten how flat and toneless her voice was. I could not see her face very clearly in the darkness but she did not give the impression of being thrilled at our meeting. I should have kissed her as soon as we met but I felt that the moment had passed.

I said, "Shall we have a drink? The Bull's Head again?"

"All right."

I felt for her hand. She was wearing furry gloves but I took it all the same. "Come on, let's get out of the cold."

I tried to hold off the slight sense of anti-climax and disappointment that was beginning to press down on my spirits. We did not seem to be the same two people who only three nights ago were pressed together in mutual delight, kissing and caressing without inhibition.

I said, "I've been longing to see you again."

"Have you?" She sounded politely interested, as if I had said I'd been given a new tie.

Perhaps a drink would help. Certainly it had seemed to work the last time. It was as well that I had enough money to see us through the evening, over seven shillings. Then I remembered that I owed Sally more than that. I decided that I would forget that uncomfortable little matter for the time being, and I hoped that she had forgotten it too.

"Did you have a good Christmas?" she asked.

I thought of the sad parody of a festive meal on Christmas Day, the chicken pretending to be a turkey and the Old Man complaining that the sprouts weren't properly cooked, the cheap crackers being pulled and Sylvia alone showing any signs of enjoyment. "Not bad," I said. "Did you?"

"Lovely."

"My brother and I got a couple of new records. *On Hearing the First Cuckoo in Spring*. Do you know it? Delius. And Rubinstein playing Chopin."

"Bertie gave me these gloves," she said.

We did not say much more until we were inside the Bull's Head saloon bar. It was not crowded tonight, just three middle-aged men sitting on high stools at the bar counter and an RAF officer and his girlfriend or wife sitting at one of the tables. The table of our last visit was vacant and by unspoken consent we headed for it and when Sally was seated I went to the bar and returned with our drinks.

She was wearing the same coat and I could see a yellow paisley scarf or cravat at her throat. When I looked straight into her face, all trace of the earlier disappointment vanished. The coldness of the night had polished her eyes to a jewelled yet liquid brilliance and brought a soft glow to her cheeks.

I said, "You look lovely."

The now familiar composed little smile moved her lips and there was a tiny glint that might have been mockery in her eyes. Then she said, "So do you."

I was a bit disconcerted by this for a moment, but I

131

recovered and said, "No, I mean it. You really do. You look marvellous."

"I mean it, too." Her voice was still without evident feeling, even-toned and matter-of-fact.

I decided to assume that she was joking and began to tell her about my arranged contest with Teakle. She seemed unsurprised by my boxing and no more or less interested than in any of the other things I had spoken of.

"I've got to get down to some hard training. He's a tough opponent," I told her.

"Robin Mander used to box at Repton," Sally told me.

"Who?"

"Robin Mander."

With an effort I restrained myself from snapping out an irritated and sarcastic comment. "Who is Robin Mander?" I said carefully.

"A friend of Bertie's."

"And of yours?" I spoke with unconcealed jealousy.

She gave a short dismissive laugh. "Of course not. He's a silly boy. He never talks about anything except motor cars."

I thought with both excitement and uneasiness that I had stepped out of my class in taking up with Sally. A friend of her brother's had been to a public school, institutions of which I had only read in biographies and novels. He almost certainly owned at least one of the cars he was always talking about.

I said, "It's not quite the same thing."

"What isn't?"

"Public school boxing. They're raw novices. They wouldn't stand a chance with a club boxer."

Sally did not seem either impressed or interested by this so I decided to try another topic. We spoke about films and their stars, a little about the progress of the war, a subject on which her ignorance equalled mine, and about books, though it must be said that I did most of the talking here. And then we hit upon a theme which seemed to possess a real grip on her interest: dogs. We arrived circuitously at this topic. I had asked her if she had read anything of interest over the Christmas holiday and she had said that she hadn't had the time.

"Why?" I asked. "What kept you so busy?"

"Oh, I had to help Mummy. Endless washing-up and then getting the next meal ready. You know. Games and things. And I had to take Bessie for long walks."

"Bessie?"

"She's an Airedale. She's lovely."

This was the start. We went on to talk about dogs we had known in the past. I spoke at length of my uncle's alsatian, Major, who had seemed to me, at the age of eight, to be the size of a small house. Sally spoke of a cocker spaniel, Bessie's predecessor, who was very fond of beer. We talked about dogs we would like to own and dogs we would never consider owning; we compared breeds and their characteristics, and Sally grew quite animated on the subject of canine diet and training.

I said, "I'd like to meet Bessie."

"You must come home with me one weekend. Or

come over on a Sunday for tea and we can ride back together on the bus."

I agreed that this sounded a good idea but the pleasurable feeling the prospect induced was accompanied by a frisson of apprehension. Would Sally's parents and her brother and sister be so uninquisitive about my age and antecedents as she seemed to be? I doubted it.

We drank three leisurely half-pints each and then Sally said she ought to head back to her digs.

Outside we began to walk very slowly, waiting for our eyes to become accustomed to the density of the night. I placed an arm about her waist and drew her close to me. At first I experienced a little difficulty in adjusting my pace to hers, but soon we seemed to achieve a degree of synchronization and I began to feel aroused by our closeness and the brushing of her hip against my thigh. When we reached her digs we began to kiss as we had on that first occasion and I found it every bit as thrilling and she was no less ardent in her response.

Some time later, when we had worked ourselves into a lather of frustrated desire and had broken apart to gasp for air, Sally recovered enough to say, "I have to go in now."

"I wish I could come in with you," I said fervently.

"So do I."

There was a significant pause. Then I said, "Do you really mean that?"

"Yes."

I was not sure how serious either of us was being. "What about it then?"

134

"What do you mean?"

"What about sneaking me in? Would anyone know? Could it be done without your landlady hearing?"

Sally laughed. "I don't know."

It suddenly seemed dazzlingly possible.

Then she said, "Not tonight though."

I was not completely sure whether I was disappointed or relieved. "Why not?"

"Because."

"Because what?"

"Because it's the wrong time."

For a moment I was puzzled by her answer. Then the meaning — or what I was nearly sure was her meaning — unfolded in my mind, and it led to another possible revelation: it seemed that she was promising that there would be a "right time", that when circumstances were more propitious she would take me to her room and, unless I had gravely mistaken her, into her bed.

"Do you think we could get away with it?" I asked. "Would you risk it?"

"I might. You'd have to be careful, though."

"Yes, of course. We both would."

"I mean you'd have to — you know — have something with you."

Again it took a second or two for her meaning to become clear.

"Oh yes. Yes, I would."

I could see that she was smiling and I did not want her to go. We heard approaching footsteps and I could just make out the shapes of a man and woman as they drew level with us and continued down the road.

She said, "I must go."

I kissed her and then she extricated herself from my embrace.

"Do you really mean it?" I asked, taking both of her hands to prevent her from leaving me.

"Mean what?"

I didn't know whether she was teasing or not. "What we said. Sneak up to your room."

"We'll see."

"It would be marvellous."

I pulled her close and kissed her again. It was a long, deep, probing kiss and I did not want it to end because I knew it was the last one of the evening. When at length I released her she turned to open the gate.

"When shall I see you?" I asked.

"Whenever you like."

I made a move to embrace her again but she slipped behind the gate.

"Tomorrow," she said, "same time and place," and she turned away and walked up the short garden path to the front door.

I waited until she had found her key and let herself in before I started to walk home. I was so filled with excitement that I felt physically gorged as if I had dined at a banquet of unimaginably rich food and drink and I thought that I would never be able to eat plain fare again.

During the next few days Sally and I met frequently but, although we made occasional half-jocular references to my creeping into her digs with her one night, we had to be content with alfresco perpendicular and incomplete love-making. I was supposed to be in strict training for my fight at the end of the month and I began to feel anxious about being unfit for a six-round bout against a formidable opponent.

The boxing club had shifted its training quarters from the old Castle Street Hall to a large room used for dances and other functions above the bar of the Victoria Club in Kingsbury Square. Our new quarters did not possess the same atmosphere as the old place, or perhaps the rough magic was simply fading away as other spells were woven by the more enchanting preoccupations of relative maturity. Not that my interest in boxing and the ambivalent pleasure I found in the practice of the sport were in danger of being obliterated. That would never happen. Once I had made the effort to pack my gear and go out into the cold night and climb the stairs to the improvised gymnasium I began to feel the old excitement stirring in the gut and making the heart beat faster.

As the disciplines and exhausting rituals of training grew more onerous — the skipping, the ground-work exercises for strengthening the abdominal muscles, punching the heavy bag, shadow-boxing — I found that I was enjoying the sparring and the competitive bouts themselves more than ever before. This was partly because of increasing confidence, which was the result of my growing physical strength and stamina, and partly because of the improvement in my command of the skills necessary for success, or at least survival, in the ring. The variety of my punches was still limited to the basic left jab, one-two punch, right-cross and a not very effective left hook to the body, but I delivered those blows with more authority than in the past and my straight left had become a weapon of attack as well as defence. My footwork had improved a lot and I had acquired a sense of ring strategy that proved valuable when I was under pressure. Much of the enjoyment came from the feeling of controlling the contest, of being able to outwit and outmanoeuvre an opponent, from feinting him into leaving himself open to a counter-attack, and doing all this with style and apparent ease. I don't think I could have been an exciting boxer to watch but, at that level of the amateur game, I was a difficult one to beat.

Among the other club-members my special friends were Frank and Joe Outram and Joe's inseparable companion, Phil Procter. Frank, who was a couple of years older than me, was about the same weight and of similar build and he acted as my chief sparring partner. He was a fairly good boxer and possessed a crippling left hook to the solar plexus, which, from countless hours of sparring with him, I had learnt how to avoid. He had an enviable temperament and always produced his very best form on big occasions. Joe, his elder brother, was short and stockily built so he was invariably compelled to concede many inches in height and reach to his opponents. He was not a bad boxer but not good enough to overcome these physical disadvantages and, of the scores of contests I saw him take part in, he never once emerged as winner, yet he remained cheerful and indomitable of spirit. His great friend Phil was a powerfully built middleweight and, while no exponent of the finer points of the game, he would slam over a sledge-hammer right swing that could, and sometimes did, bring a dramatic end to a bout. Unlike Joe, who would absorb tremendous punishment without ever wilting under its pressure, Phil objected bitterly to being hit and, if he found himself facing an opponent whom he could not flatten, and who looked likely to inflict painful damage on him, he would quite shamelessly lie down and be counted out.

These training sessions before the Town Hall show in January would be the last for many of the senior club members. Within the next few months most of them were called up or volunteered for one or other of the armed services. Phil Procter, I learnt many years later, was killed at Arnhem, serving with the Oxford and Bucks Light Infantry who were part of the sixth Airborne Division. Joe Outram was in the same regiment but I never found out what happened to him, or to his brother, Frank. The Outrams came from a village outside Aylesbury called Haddenham and they were simple country lads, good-natured, generous and brave. Phil Procter was a Geordie from Sunderland or Newcastle, who had moved south in the Depression to find work. He was perhaps less immediately likeable than Joe but he was funny and amiable and, in his own way, completely honest though not, it must be said, as brave as the Outrams, and I find it disturbing to think of him, with his reluctance to face a gloved attack from an adversary in the ring, having to contend with the impersonal fury of bullet and shrapnel from which there was no subterfuge for him to resort to.

Training nights were still marred for me by the Old

Man's presence. It was difficult not to be conscious of him standing alone just inside the gym watching my every movement with his peculiar grim smirk and knowing that he would be waiting at home when I got back to tell me that I had not spent enough time with the skipping-rope or that I coasted through the rounds of sparring without exerting myself. The days when he would threaten and sometimes execute physical punishment for what he deemed slackness or failure had passed, but the stain of apprehension and vague guilt still spoiled what should have been the pleasure of the event.

It was on the last training night before my contest with Teakle that Kenneth and I returned from the club to find him and Mam waiting for us with an air almost of conspiracy. They were sitting in the living-room above the studio and it was clear that some discussion had been held and, for once, it seemed that it had not been acrimonious. I knew that a pronouncement of some kind was about to be made and I hoped that it was not going to be to my detriment. At first I wondered if I had been seen with Sally and was going to be interrogated about this, but I dismissed that possibility because he did not look angry enough. His expression was one, rather, of a kind of furtive secrecy, a terrible coyness.

He said, "We've got some news for you."

We waited.

"Don't you want to know what it is?"

We nodded. "Yes."

He paused. Then, with a kind of verbal flourish, he said, "We're going to move. We're going to get a house."

I was quite surprised by his news and, after a moment's reflection, cautiously pleased. "Where is it? What kind of house?"

"Manor Road. That's off Bierton Road. It's a very posh part. Very nice houses. It's got a big garden and fruit trees and a garage."

"Can you afford to buy it?" Kenneth asked.

Mam said, "We're renting it, not buying. We thought we needed more room. The business is taking over most of the space here."

"When are we going to move?" I asked.

The Old Man answered. "Soon. A couple of weeks. It's a big house. We've got to get a bit more furniture."

"Will we have our own bedrooms, Kenneth and me?"

"We'll have to see," Mam said.

Then the Old Man said to me, "You were terrible tonight. You and Outram looked like a couple of chorus girls, dancing about and never punching your weight. And I noticed you were puffing after three rounds of skipping too. I warned you. I told you you'd got to be in top condition for this lad Teakle. You saw him knock out that fellow from Wycombe. Well, he's going to do the same to you unless I'm much mistaken. And it'll serve you right."

I said, "I'm pretty fit. Frank and I were taking it easy on purpose. No point in risking a cut or something a few days before the show. I'll be all right, don't worry."

"You're the one that should be worried," he said.

* * *

141

It was not until I was sitting in the dressing-room, half an hour before my contest with Teakle, waiting to be gloved up, that I began seriously to worry. Sally had decided she wanted to come and watch her first boxing tournament and I had been pleased to arrange a good place for her in the balcony behind the ringside seats, where she would be accompanied by Laura and her husband, who always attended the local shows when I was on the bill. Now I was beginning to feel very serious doubts as to the wisdom of allowing Sally to come. Defeat itself would be painful enough; to be ignominiously knocked out would be dreadful, but to be so humiliated in front of Sally was an unbearable, nightmarish prospect. As so often in the last minutes before going into the ring, I asked myself what on earth I was doing here, what madness had brought me to endure this ordeal, this dry-mouthed, cold-sweating torture when I could have been sitting in the saloon bar of the Bull's Head with Sally, warm, untroubled, excited but tenderly so, by the knowledge that soon we would be alone, in the darkness, kissing and caressing each other and whispering the sweet platitudes of love.

Hedley Rayner, one of the "whips" whose task it was to tie on the gloves and to secure round the boxer's waist the wide ribbon or narrow sash of red or blue, according to which corner of the ring his charge was to occupy, came bustling into the dressing-room. He wore the customary white sweater with roll-top neck and carried a pair of gloves, swinging them by the laces. In those days amateur boxers were not allowed to wear hand-bandages which were considered, for some reason, to be dishonourable

142

and worn only by those vulgar mercenaries of the game, the professionals.

"Right Vern," said Hedley. "Better get you gloved up. They're just starting the last round out there. Frank's winning hands down. I reckon he'll stop this kid in this round so we'd better be ready."

I could hear faintly from the main body of the hall the sound of the gong and, as if it were a signal to the crowd, the great swelling noise of their excitement. The gloves were tied on and I stood up from the wooden bench where I had been sitting and began to dance around, shadow-boxing.

Hedley said, "Come on. We'd better get out there in case it finishes quick."

I followed him out of the dressing-room and along the short corridor which led to the hall. We stopped in the entrance. The white brilliance of the arc lamps above the ring was tinted with the delicate blue haze of tobacco-smoke. You could see only the few spectators at the ringside; the rest of the crowd was a hoarse baying in the darkness, in which could be heard the sharper squeals of women or young boys.

Hedley had one arm about my shoulders. "Keep moving, Vern," he said. "You don't want to get stiff."

In the ring Frank Outram was moving forward, feinting and jabbing, working his opponent into a corner. I knew what his next manoeuvre would be because I had seen him perform it often before in contests and I had learnt how to deal with it in scores of sparring sessions. His flustered and tired-looking adversary, unfortunately for him, had no forewarning. Frank suddenly switched from the orthodox left-foot and hand-forward stance to the south-paw, shot out a solid straight right to the chin and followed it instantly with his sweeping left to the solar plexus. This was his pet punch and it connected with devastating effect. His opponent doubled up, fell to his knees and stayed there, gasping for breath while he was counted out. The Master of Ceremonies climbed into the ring and announced the verdict. Frank ducked through the ropes and descended the small steps in his corner and made for the dressing-rooms. As he passed me he grinned. "The Haddenham Terror strikes again!" he said. "Good luck, mate. You'll need it."

Hedley said, "Right. You got your gum-shield? You're on now"; and we made our way to the corner that Frank had just left where Jack Nee was standing on the ring apron, folded arms resting on the top rope. He guided me with a hand on one elbow as I ducked under the rope. I began to rub the soles of my boxing boots in the tray of resin as the crowd applauded the local man. I was wearing the Aylesbury Boxing Club colours, a green sleeveless vest and white trunks with a green stripe down each leg. When the noise of the spectators rose a little and carried a few catcalls and boos among the cheers I knew that Teakle was climbing into the opposite corner.

"Now listen," Jack said. "You've got to watch this lad. He's very useful but you've got the beating of him. Use your reach. Keep the left jab going. And move forward. Don't let him dictate. If you start back-pedalling he'll have you. You've got to be boss. Keep going forward. Jab-jab. Double it up. Then if you see an opening, slam in the old one-two. And don't forget. Keep your hands

144

high. Don't drop the left after you've thrown it. And keep your right up ready to block his left hook. That's his best punch. And don't forget he's got a good dig in his right too. Box him but box on the attack. Here . . . put your gum-shield in . . . you all right? Good lad."

The MC began his introductions. I should explain that the rules of amateur boxing were rather different then from the way things are run nowadays. The chief difference was that the referee did not officiate from inside the ring. He sat outside with two judges, each of the three posted on a raised seat at a different vantage-point round the ring. Unlike the amateur practice of today the referee kept a score-card and acted as judge as well as controller of the bout, though his verdict was not required unless the two judges arrived at different decisions. In that case the referee had the "casting vote". The terms "majority" and "unanimous" decision were not then in use, though, in effect, a "casting vote" verdict was the same as the "majority decision" of the present. Amateur boxers of today would find it difficult to understand how a bout could be refereed from outside the ring but in fact it seemed to work quite well. If an infringement of the rules had been committed — holding in a clinch, use of the head, hitting with the inside of the glove, a low punch and so on — the referee would shout, "Stop boxing!" Both boxers would immediately drop their hands and step back while the official delivered his magisterial rebuke, and then he would say, "Box on!" and the fight would continue. If one of the contestants was taking too much punishment, exactly the same command of "Stop boxing!" was issued and the referee would send the boxers back to their corners and the fight would have ended on a "technical knock-out" or stoppage. With the referee outside the ring there was no preliminary calling of the boxers together for a pre-fight homily and formal touching of gloves. The old method was for the boxers, at the sound of the bell for the first round, to meet in the centre of the ring, touch gloves, step back and then box on. The touching of gloves was repeated at the beginning of the final round, provided of course that the contest lasted that long.

The MC left the ring, bending slowly and laboriously to climb through the ropes. At this moment, a second or two before the fight began, the stifling weight of nervous tension fell away, and I became all purpose, conscious of nothing — not the noise of the crowd or Jack's last muttered exhortations, or even Sally's presence in the darkness of the hall — of nothing except the opponent in the opposite corner who I knew would be feeling exactly the same as I was feeling. The time-keeper called, "Seconds out of the ring, first round . . ." and the bell clanged.

Teakle was an inch or so shorter than I, compactly built, with the clearly defined musculature of the fully developed athlete. Intent on following Jack's instructions I moved forward, stabbing out the left, but Teakle slipped the blow adroitly, moving inside the jab and countering with a right aimed at that vulnerable area just below the heart. Instinctively my left elbow had tucked in and moved down to block his punch and I hooked with my right, missed and grabbed both of his arms in a clinch.

"Stop boxing!" the referee barked.

We lowered our gloves and waited.

"Bain. You're holding. Box on!"

Teakle jumped in at once with a left jab but, with my longer reach, I landed my own left first and followed it with a right to the body which he blocked. Each of us was trying to wrest the initiative from the other. He was striving to minimize his disadvantage in height and reach by bobbing and weaving as he launched his attacks to head and body while I was intent on preventing him from getting set to throw his combinations by constantly pressing forward with the straight left and following right. We fell into another clinch and again the referee warned me for holding. At the command to box on I threw a one-two combination, putting as much weight as I could into the short right following the measuring left jab. Neither blow connected. Teakle must have slipped beneath both punches. There was a crimson flash inside my skull and a synchronous explosion, that was both silent and deafening, and then darkness flooded in. I don't suppose I was unconscious for more than a couple of seconds. When I opened my eyes I was looking into the icy dazzle of the arc lamps. I rolled over onto my side and climbed up onto one knee. The time-keeper was counting: ". . . four, five, six . . ." I stood up at "seven" and the referee called, "Box on!"

I was distantly aware of the excited noise of the crowd as Teakle came forward. I could tell from the ache in my right jaw that he had hit me with his left hook. I kept my gloves high, elbows tucked well in and the right hand ready to block or counter a repetition of the punch that had floored me. He probably thought I was still dazed

147

from that knock-down and that all he had to do was land one more solid blow, so he moved forward without much regard for his own defence and I was able to land a solid left jab and a following right to the ribs which made him grunt. He threw his left hook again but this time I slipped inside it and landed again to the body. For the rest of the round I kept stabbing out the left jab and I succeeded in avoiding being caught by another damaging punch.

Back in the corner for the minute's rest, Jack squeezed cold water from the sponge over my head and neck and then held the water bottle to my lips so that I could rinse my mouth, and all the time he kept up a hoarse chant of encouragement and advice: "You're doing fine, son. You're boxing like a champion. Never mind about the knock-down. You won the round. Keep it up and you'll walk it. Jab and move. Jab and move. You get the chance, throw your right inside the hook. Try your left lead downstairs. Bring his guard down, then crack him on the chin. Don't take chances. Don't try and mix it. Box him. Jab and move, jab and move."

The rest of the contest must have been fairly unexciting for those in the crowd, probably the majority, who had come to see dramatic violence and bloodshed. I managed to prevent Teakle from landing another really solid punch and, though I was forced to take a few jabs and some thumps around the ribs in bouts of infighting, I kept connecting with the straight left to the head and occasional rights to the body. In the last minute of the last round Teakle launched a final and perhaps desperate attack but I wasn't going to be lured into a slugging match from which I would almost certainly emerge as the loser, and when the final gong sounded and the MC collected the judges' score-cards I was announced as the winner. A local business man, a patron of the boxing club, presented me with my prize, a canteen of cutlery, and I left the ring.

There were no showers in the Town Hall dressing-rooms so I had to make do with a cold wash at a rather grimy sink before I hurriedly dressed and went back into the hall to find Sally. I had to wait until the lights came up in the body of the hall at the end of the contest that was in progress before I could join her. Laura and her husband congratulated me on my win and I asked Sally if she wanted to stay and watch the rest of the fights or whether she had seen enough and was ready to leave. She said she would rather go so I told her to head for the exit and wait for me in the foyer while I collected my boxing kit from the dressing-room.

"I won't be more than a couple of minutes," I promised.

Back in the dressing-room I stuffed my sweat- and water-soaked gear into the battered imitation leather attaché case that I had used for years, put on my overcoat, tucked my canteen of cutlery under my arm, and made my way towards the exit. I hesitated briefly before pushing open the swing door and looked back at the ring, the taut white ropes, the canvas in the brightness of the arc lamps and I knew that, a year ago, nothing would have persuaded me voluntarily to leave before the last fight was over and, for a moment, I felt a small, perplexing sadness, a sense of loss, even of treachery. Then I turned away and went out into the foyer where Sally, whose magic was stronger than any other, was waiting for me. So was the Old Man.

I felt a jolt of shocked surprise that caused a quick intake of breath. Sally stood, looking neat and pretty and entirely composed in her smart camel-hair coat. I did not know whether they had spoken to each other, but it didn't look as if they had. I guessed that he must have seen me when I had joined her after my fight and followed her when she headed for the exit.

He said, "Where d'you think you're going?"

I knew that I was flushing with embarrassment.

"I'm taking Sally home."

"And not staying for the rest of the show? You're not interested how anyone else gets on. The lads in the club, your pals. They don't matter. Isn't that right?"

"Sally's got to get back. I can't let her go on her own."

She was watching us with mild interest and there might have been, though I could not be sure, a touch of amusement in her gaze.

"And who is Sally?" the Old Man said, glancing at her, then back at me.

"A friend." Then realizing I couldn't get out of introducing them to each other, I added, "Sally Herbert. This is my father."

She smiled and said, "How do you do."

Her composure seemed to disconcert him and he opened his mouth as if to say something but closed it without speaking and gave her an awkward, stiff nod of acknowledgement. Then he turned towards the entrance to the hall, from which the crowd noises could be heard rising and falling, and said over his shoulder as he went back inside, "Don't be late then!"

I took Sally's arm and went out into the night. We were too late to get a drink so there was nothing to do but go back to her digs.

She said, "Your father looks very young."

I hoped she wouldn't start doing sums. "He's older than he looks. How did you like the boxing?"

"It was all right."

"You don't sound very excited about it."

"It was very noisy."

"Yes. Fight crowds are."

We walked on a few yards and then she said, "Why did you fall down?"

This took a little time to digest. "You mean in the first round? I was *knocked* down. I didn't *fall* down."

"Oh, were you?"

"You mean you didn't see? He hit me with a left hook. I still feel it."

"Does it hurt?"

"A bit."

"Poor darling."

We stopped and I put down my case and the box of cutlery and kissed her. I said, "That's made it better."

We continued on our way. Then Sally asked, "What's a left hook?"

I began, "It's when you throw your left, not straight, like a piston but . . . oh, never mind."

I had hoped to impress her with my skill and toughness in the ring but clearly she had seen nothing other than two young men performing quite meaningless antics on one surface of a large roped cube. My disappointment did not last long. After all, I told myself, not many women like boxing and the few that did had no real understanding of it and were probably drawn to the spectacle for disreputable reasons.

When we reached her digs and began our ardent but inconclusive love-making the excitement of the whole evening, the thrill of victory and the relief of survival, seemed to intensify libido and I groaned even more deeply than usual with the frustrated desire for consummation.

I said, "Oh God, Sally. I want you so much! Take me in with you!"

While she seemed just as keen as I on the kissing and fondling she somehow gave the impression of retaining her self-possession.

"We can't," she said. "Mrs Sturrock'll be bound to hear us. She's always snooping and peeping out of her door when you go upstairs. But we could go away somewhere. One weekend."

"Go away? You mean . . .?"

"A hotel. A pub. Anywhere we wouldn't be likely to meet someone we know."

The beautiful simplicity of this proposal was dazzling. A night together in a hotel room, in a bed, both of us naked, all night, making love. It was at once enticing and a little frightening. I had never stayed in a hotel in my life. Could we possibly get away with it? Would they accept us as a married couple or would we be turned away, denounced, shamed?

I said, "Do you think we could?"

"Of course. Why not?"

"Where would we go?"

"Anywhere. No need to go too far, as long as it's somewhere we wouldn't bump into people who'd recognize us."

I suddenly realized that I must be giving Sally a distinct impression of timidity and youthful inexperience.

"What about London?" I said. "Not likely to meet people who know us there."

"Hardly worth going that far. We both work till six o'clock on Saturday. We could just get off at one of the stations on the way to Baker Street — Rickmansworth, somewhere like that."

"All right. When?"

"Not this weekend. Mummy and Daddy expect me at home. I could tell them I'll be staying in Aylesbury the weekend after, going to a dance or something."

It struck me then that I, too, would have to invent an excuse to explain my absence for the weekend, and that it would not be easy. But I would worry about this nearer to the time.

"What a marvellous idea," I said. "You're a genius, Sally. I can hardly wait. And I love you."

About half an hour later I released her from my reluctant arms and she went into her lodgings and I returned to Kingsbury Square where everyone had gone to bed except for the Old Man who was sitting at the table smoking a cigarette and evidently in a state of some agitation.

I was barely inside the room when the interrogation began.

"And where have you been?"

"I told you. I was taking Sally home."

"Where does she live?"

"Buckingham Road." I was suddenly aware of a hot dryness that seemed to extend from my throat down into the chest and stomach. I had often experienced this feeling of dehydration after the strenuous exertions of a fight. "I've got to get a drink of water," I said and went to the kitchen and rinsed out one of the cups on the draining board, filled it from the tap and emptied it in one long draught, refilled it and returned to the living-room. I sat down at the table and put my cup of water down in front of me.

He said, "It'd take you no more than twenty minutes to get to Buckingham Road and back here. Look at the time. Quarter-past eleven!"

I didn't say anything.

"Well?"

"Well what?"

He slammed his fist on the table-top and my cup danced and spilled water. "You insolent pup! Don't you use that tone of voice with me or you'll regret it!"

"I don't know what you want to know." I answered. "I've told you I took Sally home. We had a lot to talk about. She didn't go straight in the moment we got to the front gate."

"How long have you known her?"

"Not long."

"I said *how* long!"

"About a month."

"How old is she?"

154

"I don't know."

He got up and stabbed out his cigarette in the ashtray on the mantelpiece. He remained standing and said, "How old do you *think* she is?"

"I told you, I don't know."

He stared at me for a few seconds without speaking. Then he said, "Don't come the clever man with me. I'm trying to keep my temper. You give me straight answers or you'll be sorry. You know damn well she's a lot older than you, don't you?"

"She might be. It doesn't matter to me."

"Have you told her how old *you* are?"

"I don't think so."

"You don't think so! I don't think so either. In fact I *know* you haven't told her. Isn't that the truth? . . . Isn't it?"

I shrugged. "It didn't seem important."

"Oh, didn't it? Not important, eh? Well let me tell you it *is* important. I bet she's three or four years older than you. You're still a lad. You're only just turned eighteen. You've got no experience of the world. When I was your age I'd been in the trenches. I knew a thing or two about life. You know nothing. If you did, you'd keep away from older women. They're no good. They're poison. No wonder you nearly got yourself knocked out tonight. You weren't concentrating. Mind on other things. You were lucky to get the decision."

I decided not to argue. I hated his talking about Sally; it was as if he might leave his fingermarks on our white idyll.

"Where did you meet her?" he said. "How did you get to know her?"

I was unprepared for this. I took a drink of water. Then I said, "I met her with Alan Wilde."

"Where? How does he know her?"

"He's a friend of her brother, Bertie. And he goes out with her sister."

"Goes out with her sister! You're both kids, you and Alan Wilde, both of you. You shouldn't be going out with girls, with women. There's plenty of time for that. Alan Wilde can do what he likes. He's good for nothing anyway. But you've got a future. You could be an ABA champion. You stick to your boxing and keep away from women and keep out of pubs. If you've got to go out with girls, pick somebody more your own age. It's not healthy going out with older women."

I nodded and gave a placatory murmur of what he might think was assent. Then I had a bright idea: I said, "There's no need to worry anyway because she's going away from Aylesbury."

"Going away? When? Where to?"

"End of next week. She's got a job in London." I decided to elaborate: "She's a hairdresser. She's going to work in a posh hairdresser's in London. So I don't suppose I'll see her again anyway."

I couldn't tell whether he believed me or not. No doubt he would find out later that I had lied but I'd worry about that when it happened.

I got up from the table. "I'm tired. I'm off to bed. Goodnight."

I heard him grunt as I went out of the room and

climbed the stairs to where fantasies of Sally and me enjoying the amenities of a luxury hotel awaited and, probably, recollections of the fight with Teakle before finally sleep would carry me to the shores of another morning.

CHAPTER
EIGHT

In February 1940 we moved from Kingsbury Square to the house in Manor Road. It was a fairly large semi-detached Victorian house with a drive on one side leading to a garage which overlooked a lawn and flower-borders and peach, pear and cherry trees. At the front were two spacious rooms, one on either side of the hall, a drawing-room which contained, among other furniture, the piano, and a dining-room which was, as things turned out, rarely used for its intended purpose because to the rear of the house was a very large kitchen and smaller scullery and it was in the first of these that we usually took our meals. There were four bedrooms. Sylvia was at last to have her own but Kenneth and I still shared one at the front of the house over the dining-room though we now had a single bed each. The spare bedroom was being kept in readiness for Mam's sister, Aunt Clarice, who would be able to find refuge there if the Germans started to bomb London where she lived and conducted a small photographic business in Finsbury Park.

The Manor Road house was by far the largest and most splendid that any of us had previously lived in, yet, at first, it seemed to me that we had brought with us our own inexpungeable drabness that settled like dust over the rooms and their furnishings. This was partly the consequence of the Old Man's reluctance to pay more than was absolutely necessary for floor coverings, curtains and furniture, but it had, too, metaphysical causes. As events transpired we were not to stay there for very long and, though I was not then aware of that fact, some instinct told me that this solid, comfortable home was not intended for us. When the very early summer started in May and the trees blossomed and bore fruit the house became more companionable and acquired a kind of dim beauty, but even then I felt more like a temporarily privileged guest than someone truly at home.

But the spring and summer had not yet arrived. The war was something waiting to erupt and become real. Nothing much seemed to be happening on the Western Front. I heard on the wireless reports of British shipping being sunk by U-boats in the Atlantic and that the Russians were fighting the Finns. The war was the blacked-out windows and street-lamps at night, gas masks, ration books, identity cards and people in uniform everywhere. It was the noise of drunken singing on Saturday nights — "Roll Out the Barrel" and "South of the Border Down Mexico Way"; it was an undisclosed promise and threat, a vague excitement in the air. It was Mendelssohn's Violin Concerto in E Minor, Beniamino Gigli singing arias from *La Bohème* and *I Pagliacci*, Gershwin's *Love Walked In* and Duke Ellington's *Mood Indigo*; it was Keats's *Odes* and Orwell's *Down and Out in Paris and London*, and, above all, it was Sally and the sweet induction to the infinitely varied musics of sexual love, such moods, tunes and modulations, such multiplicity of rhythm and ornament, such harmonies, such polyphony.

Sally and I went to the Station Hotel in Rickmansworth where she had booked us a room by telephone for our weekend of love, or sex, or whatever it was. I told the Old Man that Alan Wilde and I were going to a party at the home of a friend of his and that I had been invited to stay the night with Alan. I then took the canteen of cutlery that I had received as a prize for my win over Teakle, along with some other boxing prizes — a clock and some medals and cups — to a pawnbroker's shop where I exchanged them for two pounds three shillings and sixpence which, I hoped, would more than cover the cost of our journey and the hotel room, and I bought half a dozen french letters from a barber's shop opposite the Vale recreation ground. I took with me a toothbrush, razor and shaving brush, which I slipped into Sally's suitcase. I also took my pipe which I kept gripped between my teeth as we entered the hotel and approached the reception desk, hoping that I would look mature and respectable and married. The receptionist did not denounce me as an impostor and order us both out of the place. She gave us scarcely a glance as she handed over our key and pointed to the stairs which led to our room.

Our coming together naked in a bed for the first time might have been a disappointment to us both, possibly even a disaster, but it was neither, and the responsibility for the success of a night of priapic versatility and excitement and tenderness lay wholly with Sally whose candid sensuality, complete lack of self-consciousness and — though I was too enthralled for this to be more than a tiny shadow of unease at the far edges of awareness — evident experience removed any possibility of failure. She had feared that she was about to develop a cold so she had brought with her a fresh bottle of cough mixture, and the pungent scent and flavour of this became an inextricable thread in the shimmering web of the night so that years later a sniff of Owbridge's Lung Tonic awakened fugitive erotic longings.

During the following week I thought of little else but our night of love and I wrote incoherent and shapeless rhapsodies which I showed only to Sally who said that they must be very good but she wasn't clever enough to understand them. At the weekend she went home, and Kenneth and I went out on Saturday evening to visit the Bull's Head and other pubs in town. The expedition began quietly enough. We talked about the books we were reading and we both agreed that perhaps we had overrated Rupert Brooke whose golden-haired, laughing features were beginning to pall a bit. It was all that laughter which was giving chief cause for concern. From almost every poem the guffaws came: "the laughter and the lips of light", "forget to play the lover and laughed", "the crowd's good laughter", "And laugh to laugh they ran", and we remembered that even when we were almost entirely uncritical of Brooke we could not resist mocking his "Breathless, we flung us on the windy hill,/Laughed in the sun, and kissed the lovely grass" as, on one of our walks over the Wendover hills, after a couple of pints of bitter, we recited these lines and then enacted them, hooting with affected hilarity and throwing ourselves on our faces and nibbling the grass with kisses. Yet, as we spoke of our doubts about Brooke, we admitted to a curious feeling of regret, even of betrayal, though of what or whom we were not quite sure.

After we had drunk three or four halves of Youngers Scotch Ale in the Bull's Head we moved to the Crown and there we began to talk about the war and what parts we might play in it. Kenneth had just passed his twentieth birthday and was likely to be called up at any time though his job at the laboratory might be regarded as work necessary to the war effort. We both agreed that the infantry was something to be avoided. There was something colourless, utterly unromantic about the modern foot soldier. I had seen recruits on route marches along the Hartwell road, ugly and clumsy in denim battle-dress, gaiters and boots and shapeless forage-caps, carrying their civilian gas masks in cardboard boxes because there were not enough military ones to meet the demand imposed by conscription; the young men had looked as indistinguishable from one another as were their uniforms, cropped-headed, scowling, bored, resentful. The RAF was the most attractive option, provided, of course, that one could serve as air crew. The snag here was that our elementary school background and lack of all educational qualifications would exclude us from entry unless, as we had heard rumoured, air gunners did not require guarantees of scholastic competence. The Royal Navy was less forbidding than the army. There was a slightly *louche* or raffish aspect to a seaman's dress which seemed to allow for the retention or expression of individuality in a way denied by the uniforms of the other services, and of course there were the romantic associations of ships and the sea. But why join any of the armed forces, we then questioned, when the Merchant Navy must surely be in need of sailors and would offer adventure in plenty, foreign travel, and would exact no forfeiture of our precious individuality?

We decided we would make serious enquiries about the prospects of going to sea under the Red Duster and then we talked of other things and continued drinking until closing time. When we left the Crown we did not feel inclined to go home. Our talk of a possibly dangerous future in the air or on sea had excited us and we had drunk enough to feel reckless. The Crown was set back behind the Market Square and its yard was overlooked by the back of the Bull's Head hotel at the side of which stood a block of offices. There was a fire-escape at the rear of the building and, for no other motive than a vague and rather drunken need to see what would happen next I began to climb up it, followed by Kenneth. We soon found ourselves above the flat roof of the Bull's Head with its small raised attic turrets and it was a simple matter to jump from the iron ladder of the fire-escape onto the hotel roof. I do not think that our intentions were in any way felonious, indeed I am sure that neither of us had formed anything as positive as an intention of any kind. We were simply being propelled by a childish impulse of mischief, a thirst for excitement, even for a modest amount of danger.

It was a cold clear night, the almost black sky frosted with stars and lit by a quarter-moon like a slice of luminous lime.

I said, "Thy beauty haunts me heart and soul, Oh thou fair moon so close and bright."

Kenneth said, "Shut up. There's probably somebody in those attics. They'll hear us."

I approached one of the blacked-out windows and crouched down and listened. I could hear nothing from within. I felt around the window-frame and pressed first one side, then the other. The window moved inwards sufficiently for me to squeeze my hand inside and feel for the catch which secured it to the sill. There seemed to be a heavy curtain between the inside pane and the interior of the room. I got a grip on the velvety material and tried to drag it to one side but I let go as if it had been white hot when a high-pitched squeal of feminine terror sounded from within.

I called out in what I hoped were reassuring tones, "Don't worry! There's nothing to be scared of!" but there was no response.

When I turned away from the attic window I found that Kenneth had disappeared. I prowled around for a minute or two and called his name softly a few times, without any answer from him. Perhaps he had gone down the fire-escape back to the yard of the Crown and it might be a good idea to follow him. On the other hand he might have climbed to the top of the office building so I decided to try that first. The ladder ended outside what must have been a rear fire-exit door of the office block. No sign of my brother. I stayed on the small iron landing for a few moments and then began to descend. When I reached the level of the Bull's Head roof I clambered back onto it to make sure that Kenneth had not returned to look for me. It was then that the police appeared.

There seemed to be quite a lot of them and they came across the roof at a trot.

"There he goes!" I heard one of them shout.

I wasn't going anywhere. I submitted unresistingly when two of them grabbed me by the arms. They took me down to the Crown yard and bundled me into the back of a car and drove to the police station. I was now considerably sobered and scared. The police sergeant who interrogated me was grim and completely dismissive of my claim that I had had too much to drink and had climbed the fire-escape and jumped onto the roof of the hotel simply for a high-spirited lark.

He said, "You tried to effect an entry through one of the bedroom windows. The chambermaid reported it."

I denied this charge.

"We can have you for attempted breaking and entering. Or maybe you were up to something else."

My puzzlement at this veiled alternative misdemeanour must have shown.

"Don't look so innocent," the sergeant said. "You know what I mean all right. Peeping-tom. Maybe that was your game. Scaring that young woman."

"I didn't mean to."

"Well, what was you up to then? You tried to open the window, didn't you?"

"No. Not really. I just wondered where it led to. I don't know. I was drunk."

"And what about the other man? The one that was with you. Who was it?"

I thought of Kenneth, who was probably safely home by now, with envy and some resentment. It seemed that he had deserted me and left me to face this ordeal alone.

I said, but without great conviction. "I wasn't with anyone. I was on my own."

The door of the interview-room opened and a constable came in and stood just inside. The sergeant who was sitting facing me across a table rose and joined him and they conferred briefly in low voices. The constable went out and the sergeant came back to his seat and stared at me for a moment without speaking. Then he said, "You're lying, aren't you? We *know* you wasn't alone. We know you was with somebody. We've got witnesses saw you together in the pub. And we know who it was. I advise you to tell me now. It'll save us a bit of trouble and you'd do yourself a good turn by co-operating. So who was it?"

I told myself that, since they already knew the truth, I was not behaving discreditably by confirming their knowledge, but I felt a wrench of guilt and shame when I said, "It was my brother."

"What's his name?"

I told him.

"Same address as you?"

"Yes."

"Right."

He got up and went out of the room. I was left in there with the table and two chairs, the steel filing cabinets and the single electric bulb burning beneath its white shade like a coolie's hat, alone with my fear and the sick knowledge of my treachery and cowardice. Whether or not the sergeant did know who my companion had been on the roof-top I knew that it was contemptible of me to have named him.

The Old Man drove Kenneth to the police station that night and was a grim witness of our being finger-printed and charged with attempted breaking and entering before being released to accompany him back to Manor Road. It seemed that the sheer outrageousness of our conduct had stunned him. Both Kenneth and I since early childhood had been subjected to his violent rages and assaults caused by behaviour which would elicit perhaps a mild rebuke from most adults, so we fully expected to face a rage of epic proportions, even an attempted fulfilment of his often repeated threat of swinging for us. But when we got home all he said, with a kind of heavy disgust was, "Just get out of my sight!" which, with alacrity, we did.

Kenneth and I stood trial at the petty sessions at the end of March and were bound over to be of good behaviour for a period of two years. The following Friday the *Bucks Herald* prominently featured an account of our arraignment under the headline "Men on Hotel Roof", in which we were referred to as "the boxing Bain brothers, Vernon aged eighteen and Kenneth aged twenty." The known consequences of the newspaper story were twofold: first, Sally discovered my true age, and, second, I left my job.

I saw Sally on the evening of the day on which the *Bucks Herald* appeared. She was working late and I met her at seven o'clock outside Brook House. Any slight hope that she had not seen the newspaper was dismissed very quickly.

I suggested going for a drink.

"Where?" she said.

"The Bull's Head."

"I'm surprised you've got the nerve to go there."

I decided not to question this and said, "All right. Let's go to the Green Man for a change."

She walked by my side in silence. At least she had not refused to go with me.

We found a seat in the pub and settled down with our drinks.

"I read about you in the paper," she said at once.

"Yes. I thought you might. It wasn't serious. We'd had a few drinks and were fooling about. We didn't mean to break in or anything."

Sally said, "That's not the point. I don't care what you were doing. It's your age I care about. Eighteen! You're just a child! You've been deceiving me."

"No, I haven't. I've never lied to you."

"But you let me think you were older, didn't you? I mean you knew I didn't know you were only eighteen. I'd never have gone out with you if I'd known that."

I took her hand. It lay inert in mine but at least she did not snatch it back. "Of course you wouldn't have gone out with me. That's why I couldn't let you know the truth. I was in love with you. I loved you for ages, from the first time I ever saw you. I dreamed about you. Thought of nothing but you. What difference does it make? Whether I'm eighteen or twenty-eight, what's the difference? What we've got between us, the way I love you, that's got nothing to do with time, with age. In your heart you know that. Don't you, darling? You know it makes no difference."

"We . . . ell . . ."

"Don't bow to convention. It doesn't matter what other people think. The fact that you're two or three years older than me doesn't matter a damn."

"Eight."

"What?"

"I'm eight years older than you. I'm twenty-six."

I was jolted by this information for a moment. Then I went on, "It doesn't matter. Admit it, you never suspected I was only eighteen. We belong together. I bet no one who sees us like this ever guesses there's any difference in our ages. We've been given something rare. It'd be mad to throw it away."

Sally was looking at me with a small, quizzical frown but I thought I saw the hint of a smile in her eyes, the possibility of surrender to my blandishments. I raised her hand to my lips and kissed it. "Don't leave me," I said. "I wouldn't want to go on living without you. You won't, will you? You won't leave me?"

Her smile had now displaced the frown. "I don't expect so," she said.

The reactions at the office to the story in the *Bucks Herald* varied from Laura's head-shaking, whatever-next wonderment to Albert's jokey references to Raffles, though his grin, too, was a little puzzled. Mr Harris said, "I don't know what Mr Baker's going to say about it. He's coming over on Wednesday. I expect he'll want to talk to you. He'll have read about it in the *Herald*. I know he takes it every week."

When Wednesday came and Mr Baker arrived at about ten o'clock in the morning I sat at my desk waiting for the summons which I knew would come. I did not have long to wait. A buzz sounded from the little switchboard; the number four, which meant that the call was coming from Mr Baker's office, clicked into view and I lifted the receiver of the telephone and pressed the switch to make the connection.

He said in his quick, nervous voice, that always sounded so peremptory, "Come up to my office at once, please."

I said that I would, and replaced the receiver and flipped up the switch.

"Don't worry," Laura said. "His bark's worse than his bite."

"I'm not worried," I told her, and it was true.

I climbed the two flights of stairs and knocked on his door and went in. He was sitting behind his desk and I saw that a copy of the *Bucks Herald* lay in front of him. He did not ask me to sit down so I had to stand before him like a schoolboy being carpeted.

"I've been reading about your — ah — escapade," he said. "I notice it mentions your place of work. That doesn't reflect very favourably on the firm, does it?"

What happened next surprised me at least as much as it surprised him. I said, "It shouldn't really affect your business. I hope it doesn't. I'm leaving, in any case, to join up."

"Oh." Then he asked, "When did you decide to do this?"

I thought it better not to answer truthfully that I'd made the decision ten seconds ago.

I said, "I've been thinking about it for some time."

"When do you want to go?"

"As soon as possible."

"I see." Then he said, "I think it was agreed when you joined us that a month's notice would be given on either side if you were to leave."

I waited.

"I take it you don't wish to work out the month?"

"I'd rather not."

He nodded a few times as he made a low, protracted murmuring noise before he said, "I expect we can manage without you for a week or two before we find someone else. That is if you really must leave us. You don't have to, you know. This nonsense in the *Herald* will blow over in a few days."

"Yes," I said, "I've made up my mind. I want to leave." Then, because he suddenly looked rather old and sad, I added, "It's been a good place to work."

"Very well. I suggest you stay until the end of the week. Tidy up whatever you're working on."

"Yes." I waited, not quite sure whether I had been dismissed or not.

"So good luck to you."

"Thank you."

When I was at the door he said, "What branch of the services were you going to join?"

"RAF. Air crew."

He nodded, then looked down at the papers in front of him and I went out of his office and back to my desk. Laura looked up from her typing, her eyebrows raised, questioning.

"I'm leaving at the end of the week," I told her.

"Was he cross?"

"No."

"You're supposed to get a month's notice. He must have been in a bit of a temper to sack you like that."

"He didn't sack me. I told him I wanted to leave. I'm going to join the RAF."

"We'll miss you," she said. "You should wait till you're called up."

I sat and looked down at the files and the sheets of paper covered with Albert's neat columns of figures that I was to check for the accuracy of their casting, the petty cash book and the post book, and I felt an immense impatience for the four days to pass so that I need never enter the dim and dusty office again, yet I was aware of another feeling beneath the urgent desire to be gone, an undertow of vague sadness, a premonitory regret. I had arrived here for the first time three years ago, a callow boy, and I had grown up here, or so I thought. I was leaving something of my young self behind. What I did not know was this: while it was true that I was an inch or two taller and I now shaved every other day, in the broader, metaphorical sense I was scarcely any less callow than when I had come here for my first interview with Mr Baker and had been given the job I was now so eager to abandon.

CHAPTER
NINE

I did not tell the Old Man that I had voluntarily relinquished my job but I claimed that Mr Baker had reluctantly decided that I must leave. I had delayed telling him until the first Monday morning of my life of unemployment when we were both sitting at the breakfast table.

He said, "If you think you're going to sponge on me you're making a big mistake. You'd better get down to the Labour Exchange and find yourself a job. You can't claim dole if you've been sacked."

"I'm going to try and join the RAF," I said.

"As what?"

"I don't know. Air crew."

He snorted. "What makes you think they'd take somebody like you? You need a bit of savvy. You've got to be practical. You've got to know about maths and things like that. You couldn't fly a paper kite never mind an aeroplane."

"They took Freddy Hansen. He wasn't any better at things like that than me. He's training to be an air gunner."

The Old Man just looked at me with the horribly

173

familiar and humourless smirk, shook his head and rose from the table to leave for the shop.

It was a fine April day. The sun was clean and bright, if not yet very warm, and the blossom clustered and chirruped in the gardens of Manor Road. There was no RAF recruiting office in Aylesbury but I knew that there was one in Oxford, for I had noticed it when Sally and I had spent a day there a fortnight earlier. I counted my money and found I had enough for the bus fare and a little over for something to eat. I was to meet Sally that evening at seven-thirty so I had plenty of time.

The bus ride through the Thames Valley countryside was enjoyable, and when I arrived in Oxford I spent an hour or so wandering about the town, savouring the faintly melancholy, half-painful pleasure that I had always experienced in that place, ever since my first visits by bicycle when I was still a schoolboy. The ancient buildings, the bookshops, the college gardens, the expensive men's shops, the old inns, all represented a life from which I was, and always would be, excluded. I did not feel envy of the undergraduates, for they and the existence they led were far too distantly removed from any reality that I could grasp. These young men were almost a separate species. Yet I was touched by a feeling of loss, a sense of having been permitted to look upon the Elysian Fields, but never to enter them.

When I at last came to the RAF Recruiting Office I hesitated for a few minutes and then, gathering resolution, went in. All went quite smoothly. I told the Warrant Officer in charge that I wanted to join as air crew and he explained that I would have to undergo a preliminary medical examination here at these premises and, provided I passed that with the category of A1, I would be sent on to Cardington in a few days' time to go before the Air Crew Selection Board. There I would be subjected to more stringent medical tests as well as questioned about my general background and suitability for flying duties.

He wrote down details of my age, education (about which I lied, claiming that I had attended Aylesbury Grammar School and passed the School Certificate examination) and my last place of employment.

"Right," he said. "The MI room's that way, through that door there. Take this chitty with you and give it to the doc."

"MI room?"

"Medical Inspection. On your way. When you're finished come back here with the bit of paper he'll give you."

The physical examination was quickly over. I obediently coughed, my reflexes responded to the little hammer-taps, my heart was evidently beating regularly and I read the letters on the eyesight-test chart. Back with the Warrant Officer I was handed a buff envelope.

"All the gen's in there," he said. "You'll see the date on the travel warrant. A week on Wednesday I think it is. You report to RAF Cardington and you take those papers with you. All right?"

I felt a little breathless. Things were moving faster and more decisively than I had expected. I nodded and put the envelope in my jacket inside pocket.

"Good luck, son," he said and I was dismissed.

Back in the street I was excited by a mixture of apprehension, anticipation and a sense of accomplishment. It had been so simple. I was virtually in the RAF. In my heart I knew that I was the most unsuitable of candidates for any task that required the least practicality or understanding of technological devices and that the Old Man's reaction to my announcement over breakfast that I was going to be an airman was not without justice. But the war in the air had not yet properly begun and I had little notion of what it was going to involve. Again I reassured myself by thinking that if Freddy Hansen could be accepted and prove himself able to face the demands of training, than surely I could too. Presumably an air gunner was not called on to read charts, plot courses, or understand any mechanical device more complicated than a gun, and all he had to do was press the trigger, something not beyond even my capabilities.

I had almost an hour to wait for the next bus back to Aylesbury so I went into a pub and drank a half of bitter and ate a pork pie. Later, on my way to the bus station, I came to the New Theatre and saw a poster outside advertising a forthcoming production of *Romeo and Juliet* and I made a note of the dates and times of performances. Perhaps Sally and I could go to what would be my first Shakespeare play on her half-day off unless, of course, I had already begun my air force training.

Now that winter had passed we were able to make love out of doors and since the Rickmansworth weekend we both seemed to be possessed by a kind of erotomania.

176

My need for her signalled itself in urgent and obvious ways and was teased and intensified by her apparent superficial coolness and impassivity, which were soon contradicted by her more or less wordless but strenuous and unrestrained collaboration. Two or three times each week, if the weather was reasonably fine, we walked out of town and on to the Hartwell Road. Sometimes we went as far at The Bugle and had a drink there, delaying our love-making for the journey back across the parklands of the Hartwell estate but, with increasing frequency, we simply got down to it as soon as we left the main road and found a not too uncomfortable place beneath the oaks or elms. I always carried or wore an old raincoat which we spread on the grass to serve as a groundsheet, but more often than not, in the abandonment of our shared passion, we rolled clear of this, and I always took care before my arrival home to remove the grass, twigs, and old leaves which had often fixed themselves to my clothes and hair. It was strange that, while I usually emerged from our frantic couplings stained and damp with the dew of night and sprouting small foliage like the Green Man of legend, Sally never displayed a similar dishevelment. Her hair was scarcely disarranged and the merest brush-down would leave her looking as spruce as she usually did. I came to believe that if she were fired from a cannon through dense forestry she would land on her feet, neat and demure and imperturbable.

Her extraordinary self-containment and impassivity were at once provocative, puzzling and, to some extent, frustrating. I longed to hear her expressing the intensity of physical pleasure in uninhibited cries and sobbing declarations of love, but the most I ever heard were gasps and grunts and sighs of effort rewarded. Yet, although I did not at the time understand this, providence had been generous to me in effecting or permitting our union, for her almost complete lack of self-expression presented her to me as a kind of palimpsest on which I was free to inscribe my own romantic version of her character.

If I had expected from her a strong emotional reaction to my announcement that I had joined the RAF I was disappointed. We were sitting in The Bugle after having crossed the fields to Hartwell, with a half-hour's intermission for making love, an event which, while still thrilling, was just beginning to take on a certain mechanical aspect with much less time spent on rhapsodic preliminaries.

I said, "I went to Oxford this morning. I joined the RAF. I've got to report to Cardington on the twenty-eighth. That's a week on Wednesday."

"That's not too far away. I expect you'll be able to get home quite often."

"I shan't be stationed there, I don't suppose. I think it's just a centre for Air Crew Selection. I expect I'll be sent on to another place if they accept me."

"I thought you said you'd been accepted."

"For the Air Force, yes. Not for air crew. You've got to go through another medical and aptitude tests and things."

"Are you going to be a pilot?"

"I don't know. We'll have to wait and see."

"Bertie's training to be a pilot," she said.

"Yes, I know. You told me."

"I think you should wait till they call you up."

RAF Cardington was a wilderness of concrete and red brick. Over the grey and solid lagoon of the parade ground the Air Force flag hung exhausted in the late afternoon sunshine. From the guardroom I was directed to a barrack room which contained twenty-four iron beds, and there I found a mixed group of young and not so young men, some of whom were lying on their mattresses smoking and in some cases reading newspapers or magazines, and others who were busily establishing relationships with each other, so the smoke-hazed interior was noisy with talk and laughter. I was carrying the small case that usually contained my boxing gear and which now held shaving kit, towel, toothbrush and the Methuen *Anthology of Modern Verse*.

As I stood just inside the room looking around for a vacant bed a gingery, freckled man, who looked three or four years my senior, called from where he was sitting, "I say! Over here! This bed's free!"

Gratefully I went across to the unoccupied bed and put my case on it and sat down.

The gingery man said, "My name's Donald Bell," and he held out his hand for me to shake.

I told him my own name. I was a little intimidated by his evident confidence and ease of manner. He spoke with an assured, upper-class accent and smiled as if he were quite genuinely amused by the circumstances of our meeting.

"Where do you come from, old boy?" he said.

"Aylesbury."

"Oh yes. Where the ducks come from. And what do you do in Aylesbury? Not breed ducks, I take it."

"I used to work in an office. Accountants. But I gave it up." Then I added, "To be a writer, really."

"A writer? That's jolly interesting. What sort of writing? Not that I know much about it."

"Well, I've written a few stories. And some poetry. That's what I'm most interested in. Poetry."

"Ah. Yes. I see. Not my line, I'm afraid. Eskimo Nell's about as far as I go. Still, one man's meat and all that."

"What do you do?" I asked him.

"Reading law at Oxford, after a fashion. Pretty boring stuff actually. The law's an ass, as the Bard said. Or somebody. I'm just hoping to get through the inquisition tomorrow and forget about exams and all that."

"What happens tomorrow? Do you know what we have to do?"

"Medical first, I think. Chap I know's been through it. They test your puff for some reason. You've got to blow into something and show you've got good wind. I don't know why you need that to fly an aeroplane but ours not to reason why. Then I think they make you jump up and down or run on the spot or something and take your pulse and heartbeat or whatever it is. Eyesight too has to be spot-on. They test you for colour blindness. Then you do aptitude tests. Bit of maths or simple trig or something ghastly. I don't suppose you need to be Einstein to sit in the back of a bomber and pop away at Jerry. I'm just hoping they won't be too fussy. I'd

180

have thought as long as you have a couple of eyes and the usual number of limbs they'll be only too glad to take you."

I envied his cheerful confidence and found that my own self-assurance was diminished by it. This was the first time in my life that I was to live communally and I did not find the experience comfortable. It was obvious that Donald and many of the other air crew candidates were used to living and sleeping in groups at their public schools and they showed no self-consciousness about displaying their nakedness in the ablutions. When, after lights-out, I lay in my bed I was kept awake not only by the prospect of the following day's ordeal and the heavy breathing and intermittent snoring of my companions but by a surprising ache of homesickness, a childish need for the comfort of the familiar. I thought, too, of Sally and, in the celibate and masculine darkness, I longed for her fragrant and lenitive presence. But at last I slept and the next morning I felt refreshed and better able to face what challenges the coming day would present.

After breakfast we were conducted by a Flight Sergeant to the Medical Inspection rooms where I was subjected to and survived various examinations before being handed over to an optometrist who carried out the usual card tests and then peered into each eye through an ophthalmoscope. He then showed me a folder which held glossy sheets of paper each of which was covered with a mass of multicoloured pin-point dots.

He opened the folder and showed me the first pointillistic sheet and said, "Now I want you to look at this and tell me what you see. I mean not just a lot of coloured dots but can you see anything else. A figure, a number perhaps?"

I stared at the sheet. "No. Just dots."

"Right." He turned to another sheet. "What about this one?"

"Yes! I can see an eight. Quite clearly."

"Good. Let's go back to the other one. Can you see anything now?"

I looked again but could see nothing but the swirl of dots. "No."

We tried a few more sheets. In some I could see the outline of a number but not in others. After a while he put the folder to one side. "Did you know you were colour blind?" he said.

I did not, and I found it difficult to believe.

"You probably wouldn't have trouble with bold, primary colours but only with certain shades of green and red."

"It won't affect my chances . . . I mean I won't be turned down for air crew, will I?"

"Yes, I'm afraid you will. Your left eye's astigmatic too. So I'm afraid you'll have to forget about flying. Don't let it get you down, old chap." He was busily writing on a piece of paper which, when he had finished scribbling, he folded once and handed to me. "Give this to the Flight Sergeant outside. He'll tell you what to do next. And don't be down-hearted. Lots of valuable jobs to be done on the ground, you know."

Next I was interviewed by a rather unprepossessing officer who looked to be at least in his late thirties. He was overweight and he bulged and sagged in his uniform which, I noticed, did not bear the insignia of air crew.

He said, "My name's Flight Lieutenant Ryan." I guessed, snobbishly, that he had risen from the ranks because his voice was decidedly unposh. "I see you've failed the eye test. It's a matter of finding the right job for you in the Air Force. What's your job in civvy street? What you been doing for a living?"

I told him that I worked in an office.

"What kind of office?"

"Accountants."

"You're not qualified? No, you wouldn't be. You're too young. Are you articled?"

"No. I'm just a clerk. I do a bit of auditing and checking figures. Keep the petty cash. Things like that."

"Can you use a typewriter?"

I hesitated. Then I said, "I can, but not properly. I mean I don't touch-type. Just two fingers of each hand."

"All right. I'm going to give you a little test. Check your spelling too. Go and sit over there at that desk. Take the cover off that typewriter. That's it. Settle down. Put a bit of paper in the machine — there on your right. Doesn't matter about a carbon . . . good . . . tell me when you're ready."

I nodded. "Ready."

He began his dictation, which consisted mainly of bureaucratic jargon, spoken quite slowly so that I had no difficulty in transcribing it onto the typewriter. When he had finished he rose and walked over to where I was sitting, leaned across and pulled the sheet of paper from the machine.

He began to read aloud: "With reference to your memo

dated 29th April 1940 the percentage of the new intake for the month qualifying for further training as . . ." and then his voice sunk to a barely audible mutter as he finished his reading.

"Good," he said. "No spelling mistakes. I think we can treat this as a trade test and you'll be entered as a Clerk, Grade Three."

I did not say anything but stared at him with appalled disbelief. All my imprecise but flattering dreams of heroic jauntiness, the admiration of men and the adoration of women, had been transformed in a few moments to a reality of coarse-grained ordinariness.

Ryan must have read my expression accurately. He spoke with some irritability: "You think it's not glamorous enough, don't you? Well, you listen to me, young man. For every chap in the air you need a dozen on the ground to keep him up there. We might not get the gongs and the headlines and the bits of skirt but we're the backbone of the RAF and don't you forget it." He began to write on a slip of paper. "Here," he said when he had finished, "take this and go back to your billet. Flight Sergeant Parkinson will find you there when the rest of the intake's been through selection. Give him this chitty and he'll tell you what to do next."

I left the administration block and with some difficulty found my way back to the billet. It was empty and someone had left a *Daily Mail* on one of the beds so I lay on top of my own mattress and read, with little comprehension, about Chamberlain's resignation as a consequence of the British blunders in the Norwegian campaign and the prospects of either Lord Halifax or

Churchill taking his place as Prime Minister. After a while I began to feel drowsy and I was half asleep when the rest of the recruits returned from whatever tests they had been undergoing, accompanied by the Flight Sergeant. Donald Bell was among them. He looked excited and cheerful.

"How'd it go, old boy?" he said.

"I failed the eyesight test. Colour blind."

"Oh rotten luck! What happens to you now?"

I felt too ashamed to admit that I was to serve as a Clerk, Grade Three. "It'll have to be a ground job."

"What rotten luck," he said again but he could not conceal his own excitement and pleasure at having been, so far, successful.

I gave the slip of paper to Flight Sergeant Parkinson. He glanced at what was written on it and said. "You'll get fell in with the others for swearing-in. All right?" Then he shouted, "Quiet, you men! Stand by your beds! You're going to get fell in outside and then you'll be marched down to the dining hall where you had your breakfast this morning. You're going to get sworn in. Right? Outside! All of you. Move!"

On the path in front of the billet we clumsily shuffled and nudged ourselves into columns of three to a sardonic commentary from Parkinson and then we marched, with less than military smartness and precision, to the dining hall where the tables and benches had been stacked at one end to leave a clear space for us to stand. Already recruits from other quarters of the camp were assembled, some fifty or so of us altogether. An officer whom I had not seen before was standing in desultory conversation with a Warrant Officer as the Flight Sergeant brought us to a halt and saluted.

"Hand out the Bibles," the officer said.

The Warrant Officer and the Flight Sergeant each extracted from a large cardboard box, which I had only just noticed, a stack of plainly bound New Testaments. They then moved up and down our ranks until every recruit was clutching one. The officer then took charge.

"All right, men," he announced. "You're now going to get sworn in as members of His Majesty's Royal Air Force. You will take the Bible in your right hand and raise it like this."

The recruits, still distinguishable from one another in civilian clothing and varied postures, wore a range of facial expressions, some bashfully grinning, others almost shifty in their uncertainty of reaction, and a few totally earnest, firm-jawed and resolute, like young airmen in a recruiting poster. They all held their New Testaments in their right hands, all, that is, except for me, for the realization that I was not yet irrevocably committed to the role of Clerk, Grade Three, in the Royal Air Force had flared suddenly in my consciousness. I raised my empty right hand like a schoolboy and called out, "Just a second! I want to ask a question!" In my own ears my voice carried a slightly shrill edge.

The officer, who had just begun to recite, "You will say after me . . ." was abruptly silenced and then he turned to his two subordinates and said in a rather plaintive tone, "What's that? What's that fellow saying? What's going on, Sergeant?"

186

It was the Warrant Officer who responded by barking, "You! What d'you think you're playing at? What's wrong with you, lad?"

The assembled recruits were whispering and muttering and somebody laughed.

"Quiet!" The Warrant Officer looked very angry. "That man that interrupted! Speak up!"

I called, "It was me! I want to know. If I don't do this, take the oath or whatever you call it. Does it mean you can't force me to stay? Does it mean I'm not in the RAF yet?"

The voices of my companions rose again in wonderment and more laughter.

This time it was the officer who shouted, "Quiet, you men! Stand still and keep quiet!" He conferred for a few seconds in a low voice with the Flight Sergeant and the Warrant Officer and then spoke up again: "What do you mean, lad? What the hell you doing here if you don't want to join the Service?"

"I've changed my mind," I replied.

More muttering from the assembly.

"Quiet! What do you mean, changed your mind? What's the trouble, lad? You got cold feet? Is that it?"

"I'm not staying here. I'm not doing this. I'm not going to swear in." Instead of sounding determined and robustly defiant my voice seemed to rise with a youthful, petulant note.

The officer again briefly consulted his subordinates. Then, in a louder voice, he said, "Get him out of here! Take him over to Mr Ryan. See if he can talk some sense into the fellow. Tell him what's happened here."

Flight Sergeant Parkinson beckoned to me by pointing and waving, then indicating with a jerk of his head in the direction of the exit that I should join him there. As we left together I heard the officer's voice — "Now perhaps we can get on with the war. Right, men! . . . Raise your Bibles in your right hand, like this . . . now you will say after me . . ." — and, as I was escorted back to the administrative block, the low growl of choral recitation as the assembly swore fealty to King and Country.

Parkinson left me standing in the corridor outside Flight Lieutenant Ryan's office while he went in to describe what had occurred at the swearing-in ceremony. Then I was invited in and asked to take a seat. Ryan began by attempted cajolery and adopting a rather unconvincing avuncular attitude. He told me that he understood my disappointment at being turned down for flying duties and this reaction did me credit. We all wanted to have a crack at Jerry but not all of us were lucky enough to play an active part in the air. What I must understand was that the men on the ground were just as important. Office work had to be done by somebody and I should be proud to be doing my bit although it didn't have the same glamour as air-crew duties. When I told him that I had no intention of swapping one office job for another he began to show annoyance and by the time we parted he had reached a state of almost incoherent rage.

Shortly after one o'clock in the afternoon I left the depot with my attaché case but no travel warrant for the journey home. I had very little money so I set off walking and hoped that I would be picked up by some kind-hearted motorist or lorry driver. It was one of the first hot days of early summer. The heat and brilliance shimmered above the surface of the road and a powdering of dust lay on the hedgerows. I felt happy and buoyant with a sense of reprieve and I walked briskly along the narrow country road until, after three miles or so, I reached a main thoroughfare going south towards Leighton Buzzard and Aylesbury. Another hour or so passed before a small truck carrying a load of timber gave me a lift to Linslade which was no more than ten miles from home. My luck failed to hold and I had to walk the rest of the way, arriving at Manor Road in the early evening, hot and very tired but still feeling thankful that I had escaped from Cardington. During my long tramp I had devised a cunning plan.

The Old Man had just got back from the shop and he was sitting at the kitchen table smoking a cigarette, with a half-filled cup of tea in front of him.

"Any tea in the pot?" I said.

He watched me closely but did not answer as I lifted the teapot and gave it a little shake to make sure it was not empty. I took a cup from the dresser and poured from the pot and added milk and sugar. I sat down at the table and took a drink.

He said, "Well?"

"They accepted me," I said. "I passed the medical and aptitude tests. I've got to wait till I'm sent for."

"Accepted you as what! What do you mean?"

"Air gunner. They said the station where I'll be doing my training'll notify me when my papers have gone through. It might take a week or two, they said. There's a shortage of instructors and they've got more trainees than they expected."

I tried to appear nonchalant as I drank from my cup and then cut myself a slice of bread from the half-loaf that stood on the bread board on the dresser. I spread butter, taking care not to use too much because of rationing, and added a smear of Marmite. I think the Old Man was going to question me further about my being accepted as an air gunner by the RAF but Kenneth, who had just arrived back from work, came into the kitchen.

"Your brother's going to be a war hero," the Old Man said to Kenneth. "Hitler must be shaking in his shoes."

Kenneth looked at me enquiringly.

"I passed the tests at Cardington," I said. "They said they'll call me up when the papers have gone through." I found it more difficult to lie to Kenneth and I hoped he wouldn't ask me any awkward questions. But all he did was nod and say, "Where will you do your training?"

"I won't know until they send for me."

"Might be Uxbridge," he said. "That's where Freddy Hansen went," and he picked up the teapot, lifted the lid and looked inside.

"It'll take more hot water," the Old Man said. "Don't put any more tea in. We're getting short."

Kenneth put down the teapot and went out of the kitchen. I heard his footsteps climbing the stairs to our bedroom. I finished eating my bread and Marmite and followed him upstairs to tell him what had really happened at Cardington.

CHAPTER
TEN

The long, heartless and beautiful summer of 1940 was for me a time of Elysian delight, of rapture both physical and metaphysical. My days were spent in luxurious idleness. I read a great deal, without direction but always with pleasure: Kenneth and I managed to find Hemingway's *Fiesta* and *Men Without Women* and Graham Greene's *England Made Me* and Evelyn Waugh's *A Handful of Dust*. We were thrilled by the short stories of Eudora Welty and Katherine Mansfield and by Richard Hughes's novel *A High Wind in Jamaica*. From the Pebble Lane Library we were able to obtain the poems of Wilfred Owen edited by Edmund Blunden, and somehow we discovered Edward Thomas. But by far the most exciting and illuminating experience that happened to me during this time was my first proper acquaintance with the work of Shakespeare. This initiation occurred in a rather peculiar way.

Sally and I had been to see a film called, I think, *Men Are Not Gods*. I remember almost nothing of the plot except that one of the characters, played by Sebastian Shaw, took the part of a Shakespearian actor and, in the movie, was performing in a production of *Othello*. He was depicted as being, in his private life, pathologically jealous of his actress wife, who was playing Desdemona, and the big moment of the film was when he attempted in reality to kill her as they played the murder scene in Act V scene ii. I vaguely recall that another character in the film, who had guessed the actor's wicked purpose, yelled out a warning from the gallery at the moment when Othello was about to smother his victim, so that the scene ended at that point in confusion and the probable rescue of the actress playing Desdemona. By then I had lost much of my interest in the plot of the movie because I had been distracted and enthralled by Othello's opening speech in the bedchamber and the ensuing dialogue. I had not, until then, the faintest notion of the emotive power of great dramatic verse. I was overwhelmed by it, moved in a way that I might be moved by a major performance of a fine operatic aria. What I was longing to do was get away and find these astounding words and read them for myself.

Kenneth and I possessed one of those bulky, single-volume Works of William Shakespeare, printed in double columns of minute type on each page of execrable thin paper, a book whose forbidding presence had so far deterred me from a serious investigation of its contents. But, filled with my new enthusiasm, I effortlessly overcame my distaste for its appearance, found *Othello* and flicked through the pages until I came upon the murder scene and those terrible and beautiful lines that introduce it:

It is the cause, it is the cause, my soul:
Let me not name it to you, you chaste stars!

It is the cause. Yet I'll not shed her blood,
Nor scar that whiter skin of hers than snow
And smooth as monumental alabaster.
Yet she must die, else she'll betray more men.

I read from there to the end and then turned back to the beginning of Act 1 and, for the first time in my life, read a Shakespeare play. I found it, despite the inhospitable print and unwieldy size of the book, more compelling than anything I had yet encountered in literature. A few days later, with money "borrowed" from Sally, I took a bus in the morning to Oxford and bought myself a ticket for the afternoon performance of *Romeo and Juliet*.

The youthful Robert Eddison was playing Romeo opposite Pamela Brown's Juliet, though neither performer's name then meant anything to me. As I remember it, the production was a straightforward mounting of the play with the performers wearing Elizabethan costume. To my ears and eyes it was piercingly beautiful and I was spellbound. Eddison had a voice of quite extraordinary quality and it was perfect for the lyricism of the love scenes, and Pamela Brown, who quite soon afterwards was struck down by polio, could not have been lovelier in voice or looks as his Juliet. I rode back on the bus to Aylesbury but saw nothing of the summer countryside that flowed past because I was quite literally in a state of enchantment.

The next day I went to the library and found not only *Romeo and Juliet* in the much more readable Arden Shakespeare edition but *Hamlet*, *The Tempest* and *King Lear*. Along with these I withdrew a book by a man called Egerton Smith entitled *The Principles of English Metre* and, although I found much of it incomprehensible, I learned a little about versification and began dimly to recognize that the art of poetry, as Ezra Pound has remarked, is no simpler than the art of music. I also found, in the chapter on "Blank Verse Paragraph Structure" references to and quotations from Marlowe's *Doctor Faustus*, which led me to a successful search for the text which subsequently gave me almost as much pleasure in parts as the Shakespeare plays. Since I was spending much of my time alone in the house I could, without embarrassment, read these plays aloud and this I did, trying to model my delivery on the performances of Sebastian Shaw as Othello and Robert Eddison as Romeo, no doubt with preposterous results. All the same, it is possible, perhaps probable, that the practice of reading aloud did do something towards attuning my ear to the subtle cadences of Elizabethan blank verse and it might even have taught me more than Egerton Smith's substantial study of English prosody was able to do at that time.

It is, to me, a curious fact that, although I made no deliberate attempt to memorize any of the great speeches I was reading and re-reading, I found that, very quickly, the lines had rooted themselves in memory and even today, half a century or so later, I can still recite large chunks of the Marlowe and Shakespeare plays that I was reading during that period, although my memory for more recent reading is anything but reliable. Poor Sally had to put up with a good deal of my ravings about and quotations from Shakespeare and Marlowe but she seemed to accept these with the same good-natured impassivity as ever and she was quite happy to accompany me to the Old Vic at Lambeth to see John Gielgud as Prospero and Jack Hawkins as Caliban in *The Tempest*. In that early and golden summer we made love almost daily and managed to spend two more weekends together, the second one recklessly in a pub in Aylesbury itself. How the Old Man came to learn of, or to suspect this I do not know but that is what happened.

On reflection it is surprising that he had not discovered much earlier that Sally had not left for London, as I had told him that she was about to do some four months previously; though the fact that he himself, as I was later to find out, was being distracted by sexual liaisons of his own might be at least part of the explanation for this. On the Sunday evening following our night of love-making in our room in the Aylesbury pub Sally and I, who had spent the day swimming in the Halton Reservoir and walking in the Chilterns, came back for a drink in the Bull's Head before I took her home to her digs in Buckingham Road. I walked back to Manor Road feeling selfishly at peace in a world that was being torn apart by war. The evacuation of allied forces from Dunkirk had begun and, in a few weeks' time, the Battle of Britain would be waged against a backcloth of ironically tranquil blue skies and lavish sunshine, but I was happily preoccupied by images of Sally's naked welcomings which were intermingled with the music, and ripple and rush, the flash and thunder, lilt and flow of Shakespeare's verse. So it came as an icy shock when the Old Man appeared round the corner from Manor Road as I was about to turn into it and we almost collided, face to face.

He said, "I was just coming to look for you. Where've you been?"

We were now standing still. "I've been to Halton for a swim." I was carrying my towel and swimsuit rolled up together and I raised the bundle as if demonstrating the truth of my claim.

"I don't mean today. Where were you last night? You didn't come home."

"I stayed at Alan Wilde's place."

"No, you didn't."

It was now about half-past ten and the pavements were deserted. The air was still warm and the sky was bland and blue and star-flecked. I could smell the fragrance of honeysuckle and night-scented stock. I took a step forward to continue on my way but he barred my path.

"You were with that woman, weren't you?" he said.

"What woman?"

I saw the punch coming almost too late. It was a right swing aimed, I suppose, at my jaw. Instinctively I tucked in my chin and drew back my head so that his fist landed, heavily enough to sting quite painfully, on my left ear.

"You bastard!" I said and hit him with a short right which connected just above his left eye. It was not a hard blow. Some impulse of either fear or something more atavistically complex and inexplicable made me pull the punch at the last moment, but it still carried enough power to make him take an unsteady pace backwards. I walked quickly round the corner and set off towards home, but he followed at once, grabbed me by one arm and pulled me round to face him again.

He said, "You've been lying to me! She never left Aylesbury. That Sally or whatever her name is. She never went to London. You've been seeing her, haven't you?"

"She did go to London. But she didn't like it. Didn't get on with the boss so she came back."

"She's too old for you."

"That's for me to decide. And her."

I thought he was going to throw another punch. Although there was no street lighting because of the black-out regulations, I could see his eyes popping with rage.

He said, "You think you're a big man! You're not! You're a conceited young pup! You're not working. You're sponging on other people. You've been drinking. I can smell it."

"One drink. That's all."

"There's nothing clever about drinking. She drinks too, doesn't she? That's the kind of woman she is!"

I thought it wiser to restrain the impulse to laugh at this. I said, "I'm eighteen. I'm going to be called up any day. If I'm old enough to fight in the war I'm old enough to have a drink and a girlfriend."

I began to walk again and he followed, drew level with me and continued at my side.

"You swore at me," he said, "and hit me when I wasn't ready."

I kept a wary eye on his hands in case he lashed out again.

"You hit me first."

"You should've taken it like a man. You know you deserved it."

"Balls!" I said, before prudence could prevent the word from slipping from my tongue, but I was ready for the swinging right fist he hurled at my head and I blocked it with my left forearm then hurried my pace so that I was walking swiftly, a few yards ahead of him, when we reached the house. Inside, I went straight up to the bedroom, half-expecting him to follow me but he remained downstairs and I was tucked up in darkness when I heard his footsteps on the stairs pause outside, then pass my door on the way to his own room.

The next day he did not go to work because his left eyebrow was a little swollen and discoloured, not a real shiner but resembling one enough to prevent him from showing himself to his "sitters", as he called the customers in his studio. I left the house early in the morning and managed to avoid confronting him for a couple of days. When we did meet at the kitchen table neither of us spoke. The result of our undignified brawling of Sunday night was not so much a clearing of the air as a tacit agreement that each of us would retreat into his own private territory. The fact that this meant that we did not communicate suited me perfectly because it prevented him from questioning me about the lengthening delay of my RAF call-up.

The flawless summer continued. The peaches and cherries ripened in the garden. I swam almost daily, either in the reservoir or, when I had the entrance money, in the open-air pool in the Vale recreation ground. I always took with me a book of verse or prose, more often the former, to read while sun-bathing after my swim. I had found Yeats's 1921 volume of poems, *Michael Robartes and the Dancer*, in the Pebble Lane library and I read for the first time, "Easter 1916", "The Second Coming" and "A Prayer for My Daughter", still absorbing the poetry through the senses with very little assistance from the analytical, reasoning part of the mind, yet genuinely thrilled by it in a way that in later life was never to be fully recaptured. The pleasure I found in Thomas Hardy's poetry was no less deep but it was different in that the essentially narrative nature of most of the work and the fact that its content is usually self-referential compels a more cognitive attention if the reader is going to respond to it with enjoyment. I cannot think what I would have replied if I had been asked what "The Second Coming" was about. I knew nothing, of course, about Yeats's psychically derived ideas of The Great Wheel, or cycle of history, of the Mask and Body of Fate, or of the cone and gyre, but I found myself mysteriously moved and excited by the sonorities which were inseparable from those apocalyptic images of, for instance:

A shape with lion body and the head of a man,
A gaze blank and pitiless as the sun,
Is moving its slow thighs, while all about it
Reel shadows of the indignant desert birds.
The darkness drops again; but now I know
That twenty centuries of stony sleep
Were vexed to nightmare by a rocking cradle,

And what rough beast, its hour come round at last,
Slouches towards Bethlehem to be born?

I tried to write poems myself but, though I was capable of great self-deception in many ways, I knew that the few pieces I completed were not even competent imitations of the authentic thing. This realization, though, could not depress me for very long. Life was too radiant and rich with undisclosed promises and I believed, without the least rational justification, that one day soon I would find that I had mastered the trick and real poems would appear on the page from the tip of my pencil or pen. Meanwhile there were books to be explored, music to be ravished by, the sun's languorous caressing and its dance and sparkle on the surface of the water that welcomed me into its cool silkiness, the fragrances of gardens and fields and hedgerows, and always the image or the corporeal presence of Sally who still seemed to me to be the quintessence and embodiment of all natural beauty.

She and I managed to get away for another weekend trip to London where we stayed at the Strand Palace Hotel and went to the Old Vic again, this time to see *King Lear* and, although I struggled hard to hold back the tears when the old king, in the final scene, holds the dead Cordelia in his arms, they trickled down my face and I was mortified when the house lights came on and revealed my unmanned state, which must have been plain, despite my efforts to dissimulate. Sally, as I should have expected, was dry-eyed and apparently unmoved, though later, when asked, she assured me that she had enjoyed the play adding, to my jealous pique, that she had found Edmund very handsome.

Kenneth and I managed on two occasions to visit the Queen's Hall where the Promenade Concerts were then held and which, a few months later, was to be destroyed in the Blitz. I had never before heard a symphony orchestra except on the wireless or on gramophone records and it was not only the enfolding brocades of sound that gave delight, but I was enchanted by the display of shining and shapely instruments, some of which I could not have named. The works performed, or the ones which I still remember, could not have been better chosen for a musically illiterate eighteen-year-old: Tchaikovsky's *Pathétique* and Beethoven's "Emperor" Concerto with Clifford Curzon as soloist. I retain, too, an image of a bare-shouldered woman in a pale blue gown playing Tchaikovsky's "Variations on a Rococo Theme", her auburn head bent over the cello, her wonderful white arms and shoulders gleaming like soft ivory as she coaxed the music from her instrument. Her name was Thelma Reiss and she seemed to me not merely beautiful but divine.

I knew, of course, that Britain alone was at war with Germany and that France had fallen and the Battle of Britain had begun. I knew, too, that before long I would be dragged more or less violently from my private, self-indulgent lotus-land into bleaker and less friendly territory, but this knowledge, rather than diminishing the pleasure I found in present circumstances, added a spice of uncertainty and possible danger which seemed to intensify my enjoyment. As the long summer softened

201

into its full ripeness, which held a hint of the scents and colours of the autumn, the days began to lose a fraction of their brilliant warmth and, imperceptibly at first, the hours of daylight were reduced and darkness came earlier with its white latticing of searchlights in the sky and, with increasing frequency, the banshee howling of air-raid sirens and the minatory throbbing of bombers on their way to Luton or Coventry or Birmingham to unload their cargoes of devastation on the trembling cities below them. Then life at Manor Road changed with an explosive abruptness.

The Luftwaffe was now pounding London night after night as well as making occasional daylight raids. Aunt Clarice arrived in Aylesbury in search of sanctuary at Manor Road. Neither Kenneth nor I was pleased to see her. I remember her at that time as a sour and unattractive elderly woman, though I now realize she could not have been more than in her mid to late forties. When we were small children she often spent her holidays and weekends with us at Skegness during a period when the Old Man was working as a beach photographer, also in Beeston and, later, in Aylesbury. I do not recall her as looking any younger in those days though she did seem to be more high-spirited and energetic and I remembered her being keen on swimming. On those earlier visits she was often accompanied by different men, whom Kenneth and I were instructed to address as "Uncle" so I later understood that, although she never married, she enjoyed, if that is the right word, quite a few *affaires* and was regarded as being, in the vernacular of the day, a "fast" woman. She showed no interest at all in Kenneth and me, displaying towards us an attitude of faint distaste and impatience.

Aunt Clarice had been staying with us for only a couple of weeks when one night, at about ten o'clock, the air-raid sirens wailed out their mournful warning and, soon after, the noise of anti-aircraft guns was heard and, behind their urgent thudding, the drumming sound of heavy bombers' engines. I was in the kitchen with Clarice, Mam and the Old Man. Sylvia, I suppose, was in bed and Kenneth was out at the cinema. The German raiders frequently passed over Aylesbury on their way north to the industrial targets of the Midlands, and occasionally a bomb had been dropped on the surrounding countryside but never on the town itself; until that night. We were sitting round the table with our cups of tea or cocoa when the bomb fell. Somewhere out in the darkness a great, tearing explosion shattered the relative calm of the night and the windows of the kitchen shuddered and we felt the floor, too, tremble beneath our feet. Within a few seconds Sylvia's frightened calls were floating on the echoing wake of the bomb's detonation and she came running down the stairs and into the kitchen, bare-footed and wearing only her nightdress. By this time Aunt Clarice and Mam were crouching beneath the table where Sylvia joined them. The Old Man wore a curious look of affront as if he had been insulted by a dangerously powerful bully of whom he was afraid. I sensed his fear and I knew that he realized that he had not concealed it from me. I felt more exhilaration than fear and I saw his expression change as he recognized this, and the stare he directed towards me contained both furtive shame and a gleam of hatred.

I do not mean, of course, that I possessed more courage than he. The Old Man had been under bombardments in the trenches of Flanders and, unlike me, had been well taught in terror and the awareness of his own mortality. I was an immature eighteen-year-old and had yet to learn that I was not immortal. Kenneth and I had been to London one Saturday night to "see the Blitz" as if it were a grand firework display.

I said, "I'm going out to see where it dropped."

Nobody spoke as I left the kitchen and went through the hall and out of the front door into the cool night. As I walked to the end of the road the All Clear sounded.

A large land-mine had exploded in the centre of the town and blown out a lot of shop-windows and inflicted plenty of damage on property, but there had not been many people on the streets at that time of night and consequently casualties were few. A couple of nights later three smaller bombs were dropped harmlessly in fields near the Oxford Road. This happened quite late, around midnight, when we were all in bed. We were awakened by the sirens' warning howls followed a little later by ack-ack gunfire and then the distinctive throb of the Dornier engines. The noise of the exploding bombs sounded fairly innocuous, like three deliberate thumps on a deadened big drum before the rest of the band begins to play. I heard the voices and footsteps of Mam and her sister and Sylvia as they descended to crouch under the kitchen table or in the well of the stairs, but Kenneth and I stayed in bed, and shortly afterwards, when the drone of the bombers had faded away, the All Clear sounded.

204

In the two weeks that followed no more bombs were dropped on or near Aylesbury, though there were warnings from the sirens and we heard the bombers passing over on their missions of destruction and, later, returning to their base. Aylesbury was a safe area, but not safe enough for Mam. During that fortnight arrangements were hurriedly made to sub-let the house in Manor Road. She and Sylvia packed cases and left for an even safer refuge somewhere in the Cotswolds. Aunt Clarice went with them but did not stay long, though when and why she left her sister and niece, or where she went to from there, I have never known. The Old Man, Kenneth and I returned to the flat above the shop in Kingsbury Square. What I have always thought of as the idyllic long summer at Manor Road was over.

Life at the flat was grim and I recall it now as continuously cold and crepuscular. Kenneth and I were back in that old double bed in the barely furnished rear room. None of us knew how to cook anything more demanding than a boiled egg. The Old Man ate lunch at a restaurant in the Market Square while I had pie and chips at Jack's Snacks. In the evening we made do with bread and cheese and jam. Sally was shocked by the paucity of my diet and often insisted that I ate a sandwich in the Bull's Head when we went there for a drink in the evening. The nights had grown cold and our walks across the fields to Hartwell and the interludes of love-making became less frequent and were finally abandoned. Now that I was spending far more time in close proximity to the Old Man than in the Manor Road days he seemed suddenly to become aware of the idle nature of my existence and I am sure that he suspected that the story of my standing by to be called up by the RAF was a lie.

One morning after Kenneth had left for work the Old Man said, "And I suppose you're going to hang about doing nothing all day." When I didn't answer he went on: "I'm going to get in touch with the Air Ministry and find out about your so-called enlistment. I don't know what you're up to but I know one thing. If they'd accepted you — and I never believed they would — you'd've been in uniform long before now. So you get yourself a job and start earning your keep."

Finding a job was not difficult because of the shortage of young men on the labour market due to conscription. A large garage called the Aylesbury Motor Company employed me in their stores selling spare parts and accessories, an occupation for which I was totally unequipped since I knew nothing at all about cars. Fortunately for me I was not the only person working in the stores. My superior was an older man called Joe who was a boxing enthusiast and well disposed towards me so, except for the periods when he was away for his lunch break and I was left in charge, he protected me from revealing my complete ignorance of the working parts of the internal combustion engine by keeping a sharp eye and ear on my transactions with customers, even though he might be serving someone himself, and steering me towards the items requested. When I was left on my own I found that the easiest way to deal with people asking for spare parts was to tell them that I was not the storeman but simply keeping an eye on things while he was out for lunch and suggesting that they came back later. My employers did not receive much from me in return for the wages of thirty-five shillings a week, though it seemed to me that I was ill compensated for the hours of boredom which I endured daily. I consoled myself with the thought that I would not have to put up with these circumstances for very long, for I would soon be swept away into the maelstrom of the war, though I had no clear idea then of how this was going to come about.

CHAPTER
ELEVEN

The hours of daylight were reduced, the weather grew still colder and the German bombers continued to fly over the searchlight-probed skies above Aylesbury almost every night. Whether or not the Old Man heard any news of Sylvia and Mam he conveyed none to Kenneth and me. He did not spend much time in the flat after he had finished work for the day and almost every evening he went out, sometimes saying, "I'm off to the Con Club for a game of billiards", as if we cared where he was going or what he was going to do when he got there. That he was prompted by guilt to offer us these muttered explanations of his often lengthy absences did not occur to me until one evening, an hour or so after he had left for his alleged visit to the Conservative Club, the telephone rang and I answered it to hear a woman's voice.

"Is that you, Jim?" she said.

Without hesitation I answered "Yes."

Clearly the speaker at the other end of the line was expecting to hear the Old Man's voice and my single syllable aroused no suspicion of my identity. She at once launched into a flood of reproach and recrimination, sounding both angry and close to tears:

"Why didn't you come last night? I waited in all evening. I'd got some off-the-ration ham, too. I made us a meal. How could you! You promised! Where were you? Why didn't you come? I know where you were. You were with that bitch, weren't you? Admit it! You were with her! I know you were . . . Jim! Why don't you answer me? You're ashamed to, aren't you . . . Jim! . . . Say something . . . I know you're there! . . ."

I replaced the receiver on the hook of the tall telephone which was rarely used for any purpose other than business, and waited to see if it would ring again. It did not. My first reaction to the call was one of confusion, but this receded fairly quickly as, not only the immediate situation, but events of the past involving the Old Man and his associations with women took on a less ambiguous significance. I had not thought of him until that moment as a man capable of feeling any passions other than those of rage and hatred. I had never seen him show signs of affection for his wife, or even for his daughter, and his very rare and usually oblique references to the existence of sexuality had always been informed by a sour repugnance as if the whole business repelled him. But I began to recall things that had been strange and disturbing enough to be stored in the darker folds of memory until they could be released by such a moment of sudden illumination as this telephone call supplied.

Images from the past which, when they had occasionally drifted into view, had been blurred as if seen in a mist suddenly came into sharper focus, bringing at first incredulity, then amazed recognition. I remembered one summer evening when I was about eleven years old and Eddie MacSweeney and I were walking back from the old recreation ground where we had been playing cricket. As we came into Market Square Eddie had said, "Look! There's your dad. Getting into that car."

On the far side of the Square, near the King's Head Hotel, I saw the Old Man bending forward to look into a green saloon car which was parked at the kerb. He was speaking to the driver and I thought for a moment that he might be giving directions to someone strange to the town, but a second later he opened the car door and climbed in and took the passenger seat. We watched the car move away and turn in our direction. It passed us, going quite slowly, and I saw that he was being driven by a woman I had never seen before. The car turned into Walton Street and disappeared.

"Who was he with?" Eddie said.

I told him I didn't know and I felt a small frisson of excitement. She might be someone I would meet later, a previously unknown aunt, perhaps, who would bring a brief sparkle into the gloom of life at Kingsbury Square and might even give us children a gift of some kind before she went away. When I got home I told Mam that I had seen my father in a motor car with a woman and I asked who she was and if she would be coming to see us. I don't recall that Mam displayed any obvious distress or anger but later that night I was awakened by the sounds of a more than usually acrimonious quarrel coming from downstairs and I knew that the row was, in some way that remained concealed from me, connected with the woman in the car.

A couple of years later another puzzling and obscurely disturbing incident occurred involving a strange woman. This was in the winter and members of the Aylesbury Boxing Club were travelling in a hired coach back from Barnet where we had been competing against the local club. Journeys of this kind were usually enjoyable occasions. Along with the junior and senior boxers came the trainer and club officials with a few supporters, including the Old Man. These trips were always entirely masculine affairs. On the way back there was a lot of ribaldry and laughter and singing. The older travellers refreshed themselves with bottled beer and we youngsters were given Tizer and toffees or chocolate. The Old Man, always and to our great relief, sat apart from Kenneth and me, usually managing to secure a seat next to one of the more respectable or affluent members of the committee, and when the singing began he, of course, never joined in but sat with his mouth tight and down-turned in the familiar smirk of superior amusement and contempt. On the return journey from Barnet the atmosphere in the coach was quite different from the usual one of slightly bibulous heartiness and sentimentality. The laughter was less robust and, with the reduction in volume, came a sly, almost furtive note. There was some whispering and nudging and a few glances of what looked like a mixture of pity and amusement cast in the direction of Kenneth and me. The reason for this change was that a woman was now on the coach and, since all the seats were occupied, she was obliged to sit on the lap of the person who had brought her on board, the Old Man.

Where he had found her was, and still is, a mystery

and why she should be travelling to Aylesbury was also inexplicable. I cannot remember much about her except that she had dark hair, looked quite young and she seemed to be laughing a lot and enjoying the trip. When we arrived in Aylesbury at about midnight Kenneth and I left the coach and were about to set off for Kingsbury Square when the Old Man called to me from where he was standing on the pavement in the light from the stationary coach windows. I went back to him. I thought I could just see the woman waiting in the darkness of a nearby shop doorway.

He said, "I'll be back later. I've got to get the car out and give, ah, give a lift home. Somewhere near Tring. No need to say anything to your mother. If she wakes up just say I'll be back shortly."

I don't know whether Kenneth understood what was going on and chose not to talk about it. I was aware of an uneasy feeling that I could not quite identify, a faint whiff of corruption and mendacity in the air, and I know I was obscurely relieved when, at home, Kenneth and I were able to get to bed without waking Mam or Sylvia.

Another and more troubling memory from a much earlier time, when I could have been no older than six or, at the most, seven years of age, was also released by that telephone call. We were living in Beeston and it was summer. Aunt Clarice was visiting, this time unaccompanied by one of the "uncles", and we all went down to picnic in the fields which skirted the river Trent. That early afternoon stays in my mind as a dream-like and idealized image of childhood summer.

The houseboats were brightly painted and their simple shapes looked like children's paintings of Noah's Ark. There was music floating in the river-smelling air above the surface of the water, foxtrots and waltzes played on portable gramophones, the jaunty, rhythmic plunking of a ukulele or banjo. We sat among the buttercups and daisies and ate potted-meat sandwiches and drank lemonade. Then Clarice, who had brought her large towel and bathing costume, said that she was going in for a swim.

She began to undress, draping herself in the towel as she discarded from beneath its cover one garment after another. Something strange, that was oddly threatening yet contained a tiny charge of excitement and mystery, was generated by her laughter and gestures. I saw that the Old Man was watching her intently and he was grinning and the look in his eyes and the shape of his mouth were very similar to the expression he had worn when he had been persuading Uncle Bob to put on the boxing-gloves.

Then he said, "I'd like a swim. Pity I haven't got anything to wear."

Clarice, who had just wriggled into her costume and let the towel fall to the grass, bent down and from the small pile of her clothes she picked up her knickers. All I remember of them was that they were of a pale yellow colour and were slippery looking, frail, feminine and shocking. I don't think I had ever before seen female underwear, certainly not of that frivolous kind.

"Wear these," Clarice said. "Go on. I dare you!"

He did not at once accept her challenge and in the

pause before he moved they stared at each other. Both were smiling but there was no levity in either of their smiles. They both seemed unaware of the presence of the other members of the picnic. The air itself seemed to have changed, become heavier with a kind of anonymous danger, a quality that alarmed and menaced like the weight in the sultry air before a storm. Yet the sun shone just as brightly on the greenness and the white and yellow flowers and the baked cow-pats.

He said, "Give us your towel," and he too began to undress beneath its modest protection. I did not watch him putting on her knickers. I got up and walked away and when I had gone a few yards along the river bank Kenneth joined me. Neither of us spoke about what had prompted us to leave the grown-ups but I now know that we had both been aware of the presence of the serpent on that summer afternoon though many years would pass before we would be able to give it a name.

It was at about the same time as the Old Man's telephone call that I received another and far more disturbing shock, this one relating to my own sexual and emotional life. Sally and I saw each other almost every evening except for the weekends when she went home to Buckingham. Tacitly and begrudgingly the Old Man had accepted her as my girlfriend and when he was out at the Con Club or, as now seemed more likely, visiting one or other of his women, Sally and I were able to make use of the studio couch for our own love-making. Then, one Sunday evening after she had spent Friday and Saturday nights at her home and was to arrive back in Aylesbury on the bus which got into Kingsbury Square at ten past nine I went out to the Bull's Head to have a drink while waiting to meet her.

The saloon bar was not crowded and I took a seat with my beer at the table where Sally and I often sat and I began to read. But my attention was only partly held by my book. At the bar counter on high stools were three young men, two of whom I knew slightly and had exchanged greetings with as I had ordered my drink, the third I knew only by reputation. His name was Kirk and he was a few years older than I and had some kind of clerical job in the County Offices. His reputation was that of a Casanova or as Albert, my former colleague at Baker's, had expressed it, "a proper lad for the girls". Albert, who had been at school with him, had spoken with awe of his successes with women and, though the accounts of his exploits had come from Kirk himself, Albert seemed to accept their veracity without question. I found them more difficult to believe because, to me, Kirk did not look like the kind of man who would attract girls. My standards of masculine attractiveness were based on the looks of popular film actors. I assumed that the kind of face that caused feminine hearts to beat faster possessed regular clean-cut features, firm jaw-line, straight nose, wavy hair and a gleaming white smile. Kirk looked shifty, with dark jowls, heavy brows above close-set eyes and an oddly secretive grin that rarely left his lips, not a bit like Gary Cooper or Leslie Howard. He was talking in a low, but perfectly audible voice to his friends and, in complete conformity with his reputation, he was talking about his successes with women. His audience seemed

215

to be encouraging him with occasional exclamations of amazement and scandalized laughter. Then I heard him say, quite clearly, the words which pierced me like poison darts and left me gasping and trembling with outraged incredulity which was almost immediately modified by painful doubt.

"Sally Herbert she's called," he was saying. "Hairdresser, works in Brook House. I was over in Buckingham a couple of weeks ago. Went to a dance there and Sally turned up with another girl, her sister I think. Not sure. I wasn't interested anyway, not in the other girl. Sally was the one. She's hot stuff, I don't mind telling you. We had a couple of dances but she couldn't wait to get outside. I had her in the back of the old Austin and she just couldn't get enough of it. I'm not kidding. She was mad for it!"

His audience sniggered.

I pushed my chair back and stood up. It seemed that I paused for some time. All movement seemed to be frozen. The three young men on their bar stools were silent and motionless, like a still frame from a movie. They were looking in my direction with traces of amusement fixed on their faces. I knew that what I ought to do was hit Kirk, knock him off his perch. That was what Clark Gable or Spencer Tracy would have done. My fists were bunched and I took a step towards him. But that was as far as I went. Something prevented me, maybe the unconscious realization that the blow would be an acknowledgement of the truth of his words. Then suddenly movement was restored. Kirk and his companions were lifting their glasses and drinking. They were not looking at me now and they were talking. I picked up my book from the table where I had been sitting, stuffed it into my coat pocket, and went out into the darkness.

The wind was cold and I shivered, yet I felt feverish and dizzy with rage and self-pity and the sick feeling of betrayal. I walked towards the Kingsbury Square bus station though I had half an hour to wait before Sally's bus would arrive. I told myself that Kirk had been lying, but I did not believe my own attempts at reassurance. I knew that I had been a fool to think that her eager sexual appetite could be satisfied only by me. Right from the beginning she had instructed and led me with an expertness that could only have been the result of experience, though I had somehow managed to avoid confronting this unpalatable fact and, had I been forced to face it, I believe I would have claimed that, after her meeting with me and our subsequent union, the past had been obliterated and I was her one true love and only possible partner. Now I knew otherwise. Or did I? Had Kirk been lying? It was well-known that men who boasted of their sexual prowess were notorious liars. Sally could not possibly have given herself to this slimy, furtive-looking brute, she who was so clean and fragrant and warm and tender. She was mine. We belonged to each other. We loved each other. She could not have done it. It was impossible. And yet the doubt remained and spread and throbbed and ached like an infected wound.

I went into the Red Lion and ordered a whisky. I did not like the stuff but a half of bitter seemed somehow inappropriate to the occasion. The pain I felt was real enough, but there was a part of my mind that was able to make the suffering more manageable by dramatizing it. I sipped from my glass and saw myself as a tragic victim of woman's deceitfulness. Then suddenly the reality of what I feared, of what I almost knew, to be true, cut through the flimsy protection of my play-acting and I wanted to howl with anguish. I turned and blundered out of the bar and began to run through the night, along Pebble Lane towards St Mary's Church. When I reached the iron railings of the churchyard I stopped and grasped them and pressed my forehead against their coldness and gave voice, not to a great howl but to little cries of pain and rage and desolation. Gradually these were reduced to occasional whimpers and groans and finally I was able to hold these down, though the weight of unuttered misery was heavy in the guts and tight across the chest. Then I went back to the Square to meet Sally's bus.

She climbed down carrying her weekend case which I took from her. I could see in spite of the black-out that she looked composed, faintly smiling, smart and pretty. We began to walk towards Buckingham Road. I had replied to her greeting with an unresponsive grunt.

She said, "What's wrong? You had a row with your father again?"

"No."

She did not seem to notice the abruptness of my answer. "You have a nice weekend?"

I did not reply for a moment. Then I said, "Not as good as you had a couple of weeks ago. And this weekend too for all I know."

Sally said nothing but this was much more likely because she had found my words incomprehensible than from guilty discomfiture.

Then I blurted out, "Do you know Ronald Kirk? You do, don't you. You know him all right. And he knows you."

"Ronald Kirk? A dark boy, works in the County Offices? Yes, I've met him."

I felt anger coming to the boil. "You went to a dance in Buckingham when you were down there the weekend before last, didn't you?"

"The weekend before last? Did I? Oh yes, I remember now, Meg and I went. It was a charity dance for the Red Cross."

"Funny you didn't mention it before."

"Didn't I? I don't suppose I thought you'd be interested."

"I'm interested all right. Was Kirk there?"

"At the dance?" She did not sound perturbed by the question. "Yes, I think he was. I'm sure I saw him. Why?"

"You did more than see him."

"What do you mean?" Her level voice seemed genuinely puzzled.

"I'll tell you what I mean. He was in the Bull's Head tonight. He was swanking about what he did with you. In the back seat of his car." I stopped walking, dropped her case onto the pavement and grasped both of her arms above the elbows, turning her to face me. She gave a small gasp of surprise or pain. "You couldn't get enough of it, he said!"

"Let go! You're hurting!"

"You did, didn't you? You and him! You did it in the back of his car!" I gave her a shake.

"Of course not."

I shook her again. "Why should he lie? Why you? Why your name? Because it's true, isn't it? You bitch!"

From as much as I could see of her face in the darkness it looked perfectly composed.

"No," she said with what, for her, was some spirit, "it isn't true. Ronald Kirk's a liar. He's a show-off. You know the way boys talk about girls." Then she said, "Let go of my arms, please."

I retained my hold for a couple of seconds, then released her. I did not know whether I believed her or not, or even if I wanted to believe her. There was something hideously but powerfully exciting in the pain caused by the thought of her and Kirk together in the back of his car, her legs wide, her small welcoming cries, that I had heard so often, now encouraging his gross entry and strenuous pumping. Then vengeful anger dominated completely and I was shaken and sickened by the urge to smash, to hurt, to destroy.

If I had stayed with Sally for another moment I think I would have directed this destructive rage towards her, but I turned away and left her standing with her case on the pavement and set off at a run, back towards the Bull's Head. I knew that the pubs shut on Sundays at ten o'clock and, if I did not crash into a stunning obstacle in the black-out, I could be back in the bar ten minutes before closing-time, and Kirk might still be there. I did not collide with telephone kiosk or lamp-post and when

I pushed my way breathlessly through the swing doors of the saloon bar Kirk and his two companions were still sitting on their stools and were, apart from the barmaid, the only occupants of the place.

I knew that I must act before reason and self-consciousness supervened. I walked straight across to where Kirk was sitting. He turned his head towards me with a vestigial grin on his mouth and a look of mildly surprised enquiry in his eyes. I don't think I could have stopped myself by this time even if I had wished to. I threw a right hook, aimed roughly at his chin. It seems likely that I was already regretting the act, for the punch carried no real power. However, it landed somewhere on the side of his face and it was probably sheer surprise and his instinctive recoil from the blow rather than the force of the punch that toppled him off his stool. I caught a glimpse of the open-mouthed amazement of his drinking partners and heard the squeak of shocked wonderment from the barmaid as I strode back into the cold darkness and headed for home.

During the next two or three days I worried a lot about my assault on Kirk. First came the more practical anxieties: would he go to the police or to a solicitor and start legal proceedings against me for what must have seemed like a wholly unprovoked attack on him? There were three witnesses, his drinking companions and the barmaid, all of whom no doubt would be prepared to swear in court that the assault had been quite without justification. I was almost sure he had not been badly hurt; the punch was light and could not have caused serious damage, but it was possible that he could have struck his head or fallen awkwardly when he tumbled from his stool. And, even if he took no action against me, I would never be able to go into the Bull's Head again. The barmaid knew who I was and I was sure she would have reported the incident to the manager and I felt pretty certain that he would give instructions that I was not in future to be served on the premises. In any case I felt much too ashamed to show myself in the place again.

I don't think my attack on Kirk would in those days have been judged quite so outrageous as such behaviour would seem today in the bar of a respectable hotel in a rural market town. Informal fisticuffs might not have been any more common then than now but the social climate, including standards of what was acceptable public conduct, was then perhaps less hostile to behaviour of the kind I had displayed in the Bull's Head. The reason why I suggest this is based on the knowledge that many people at that time took as their models for what was tolerable or even admirable social behaviour the manner and actions shown on the cinema screen by their film-star heroes. In the movies, especially those made in America, which were by far the most popular and influential, the knock-out punch was not only a necessary item in the male star's equipment, it was quite frequently used to resolve the complexities of plot, and the audiences would always applaud its vigorous use. Even now, in the last decade of the century, old black-and-white films are still shown on television and I have marvelled at how frequently the villains are dispatched by a wallop to the jaw, and that these violent *coups de main* are often

222

delivered, not as might be expected by cowboys and gangsters in small-town saloon or Chicago speak-easy, but by elegantly dressed business or professional men in drawing-room or penthouse apartment.

The Old Man was a firm believer in the heroic one-punch resolution and many of the stories he would tell Kenneth and me in the days before we grew too old and sceptical to provide the admiring audience he enjoyed ended with his not only saying ". . . so I put one on his chin", but accompanying the words and baleful glare with the crashing of his right fist into the palm of his left hand. I suppose these tales and the examples displayed by the film actors might have had some effect on the way I had behaved in the pub but I certainly did not feel that I had acted in a justifiable, far less a heroic, way. I knew that my conduct had been foolish and childish, and I was ashamed. Furthermore the suspicion and sick misery caused by Kirk's boasts had not in any way been assuaged.

I saw Sally during the days following that terrible Sunday and on the Wednesday, when the Old Man was out, she and I made love again in the studio, but it was not the same. My need for her was no less urgent but its nature had changed. The act was no longer the expression of a desire for union; the old feeling of tenderness and gratitude was absent. The violence of penetration was vengeful and after the climax came a dry, exhausted sense of emptiness followed by anger and bitterness. I questioned her again about the night of the dance in Buckingham and I tried to persuade her to admit that what Kirk had claimed was true. I grew cunning and concealed the cruel rage that possessed me. I spoke calmly and reasonably, telling her that I simply wanted to know the truth. Once she had confessed we could start again, a fresh, flawless beginning. Maybe she'd had a drink or so too many and didn't know quite what was happening. All I wanted was for her to tell me. But she said in her untroubled, almost expressionless voice that there was nothing to tell, and part of me wanted to believe her, but the other, perhaps more clamorous, part craved to be told that Kirk's story was true, that she had gone with him and climbed into the back of his car and he had pulled off her knickers and rammed his big cock into her and she had been, in his words, mad for it, unable to get enough.

When I walked with her that night to her lodgings in Buckingham Road I tried to recover something of my early feelings of love for her, but it was no good. I kissed her goodnight but her mouth felt small and dry. There must have been a moon because I could see her face quite clearly. Her prettiness no longer reached to my heart and sweetened the spaces there, and her impassivity, which had once been so provocative, now looked like mindlessness, vapid and complacent.

She said, "Will I see you tomorrow?"

"No, I'm going out with Kenneth and a friend of his. I'll see you the next day, I expect."

"The next day's Friday. I'm going home for the weekend."

"All right. I'll see you on Sunday. Off the bus."

I wondered if she was thinking of the last time I had met her off the bus, just four nights ago. If she was,

224

nothing showed in her face. I said goodnight but did not kiss her again. Her heels tapped on the path as she walked to the door. I could see the calves of her beautiful legs gleaming palely as she unlocked the door and I turned away with a sharp but momentary pang of regret. Then I went back to the flat in Kingsbury Square.

My story about going somewhere with Kenneth and his friend was untrue, an excuse to give me time to try to sort out my feelings about Sally without the distraction of her presence, but when the following evening came I found that I missed her and I began to torment myself with prurient speculations about what she might be doing and in what dark place, and with whom. Kenneth went out to see his friend Geoff Copps, who was home on leave from the army, and a little later the Old Man left and I guessed from the care with which he had just shaved and dressed himself in his best clothes that he was off to meet the owner of the voice on the telephone or someone else, her rival perhaps about whom she had sounded so bitter. I had the flat to myself but this circumstance, which would normally be cause for quiet rejoicing, gave me no pleasure. At first I tried to read. I was half-way through *The Return of the Native* and enjoying it greatly but on that evening I found that even Hardy could not hold my attention. I played a record on the gramophone pick-up — I think it was Debussy's *La Mer* — but again I found I could not concentrate, and when the first side of the disc was completed I did not bother to turn it over but wandered upstairs, first into my bedroom, where I glanced at some attempts I had been making at writing a poem, a sad and bitter meditation on the inconstancy of woman and the transience of erotic love in the manner of Dowson, or so I believed, and finding nothing here to console or encourage, I went into the Old Man's bedroom, switched on the light and began to snoop around.

I don't think I was looking for anything in particular though I suspect that I might have been hoping to find evidence that would supply proof of his infidelities, a letter perhaps or maybe something — I was not quite sure what it could be — more titillating. A quick glance through the chest of drawers revealed nothing of interest, unless a red rubber contraption with a bulb like a small old-fashioned motor-horn to which was attached a tube with a phallic-shaped ending could be called interesting. I found this object obscurely repugnant and sinister. It exuded a slight smell, rubbery, but of something else, indefinable, bitter, and hinting at putrefaction. I shut the drawer, in which it was coiled like a serpent, and turned away to the wardrobe. I saw that this large heavy piece of furniture was shut but that a small key had been left in the lock of the door. I turned the key and the door swung open.

A different smell, dusty, stale and tainted with mothballs drifted out from the rows of hanging clothes, old dresses and coats belonging to Mam, and the Old Man's jackets and trousers. There was not much of interest here, unless the pockets might hold something worth looking for. But the thought of reaching into the Old Man's clothes was distasteful and I was about to close the door when I noticed, protruding from beneath some rolled-up socks on one of the small shelves at each side of the hanging garments, what looked like the corner of a leather-bound book. When I pulled it out I saw that I had been mistaken: it was not a book but a well-stuffed wallet held tightly shut by a rubber band. I removed this and the wallet fell open. Both sides were filled with one-pound notes.

I found that I was trembling with a kind of fear, or perhaps awe would be the better word for the poignancy of the feeling that contained both the thrill of discovery and the breath-stopping temptation that these two thick wads of grubby pieces of paper brought to sudden life. I had never before seen anything like so much money, far less held it in my hands. I began to count, but gave up after I had reached ninety and was no more than half-way through the notes in only one pocket of the wallet. There must have been at least four hundred pounds tucked away beneath those rolled-up socks. I extracted one note and replaced the wallet where I had found it and re-locked the wardrobe door. I switched off the light and went downstairs and out of the flat.

First I visited the King's Head and drank a couple of halves of bitter and, reckless from my new and ill-gained affluence, I bought a packet of twenty Players cigarettes. It was by now just after nine o'clock, still time to seek adventure in the town before the pubs closed. I left the King's Head and had another beer in the Green Man but there was no one there I knew and I drank quickly and returned to the street. I crossed Market Square and entered the passageway that led to the Dark Lantern. Faint sounds of a piano playing ragtime and of talk and laughter directed me towards the pub and I felt my way along the blacked-out casement windows to the entrance and went into the smoky brightness and warmth and noise.

Among the customers were a few airmen from Halton Camp and with them a couple of girls who worked in the hat factory on the Bicester Road. One of the airmen was playing the piano with more skill than the old and jangling instrument deserved. I went to the bar and was just giving my order when I felt a hand on my shoulder and heard a voice saying, "All right, miss, I'll pay for that! And a bottle of Bass for me."

I looked behind me and saw the friendly grinning face of Ray Dixon, a young man who had come to Aylesbury from the north-east to find work and had joined the boxing club the previous season. He was three or four years older than I, confident and dashing, with shining black hair and a thin film-star's moustache. In his sharp blue suit and patent leather shoes, so narrow and pointed that it seemed impossible that they could accommodate ordinary feet, he looked as if he should be on the dance floor of some Palais or Locarno rather than in this crowded little country pub. Although he bore none of the facial characteristics of a fighter he had proved in his half a dozen appearances for the club to be a fast, resourceful lightweight, tough, courageous and equipped with a heavy punch in either hand. We had exchanged greetings and perhaps a few generalities in the club dressing-room but never more than these. I had been slightly intimidated by his apparent self-assurance and what seemed to be worldliness, and now that we were to have a drink together I still felt a residual shyness. The Old Man had referred to him, after his first appearance at the club, as "a common little tyke", which description had done nothing to prejudice me against Ray.

I thanked him for the drink and we raised our glasses and toasted each other.

He said, "Surprised to find you in here. Never thought of you as being a drinker somehow. I bet your Dad don't know where you are."

"I don't care whether he knows or not," I said and then, feeling that my disavowal had sound weak and childish, I added, "fuck him anyway."

Ray grinned. "You don't get on too well, eh?"

"No. I hate the bastard."

"Never had that problem myself. My dad buggered off when I was six. Never heard a word since. My ma brought us up, three of us, one girl, two boys. Grand woman."

We talked about boxing and he asked me if I would be going to the club this season.

"I don't know. I doubt it. I want to get away from Aylesbury. Join one of the services, I expect."

"What do you fancy? The RAF? Navy? Army?"

"I thought I'd try and get in the Merchant Navy."

"My young brother's at sea. Alec, they call him. He's a steward on the Hogarth Line. Ma gets worried sick about him."

I ordered our glasses to be refilled. Then I said, "How did your brother get into the Merchant Navy? How long's he been at sea?"

"Couple of years. He went to a place called the Gravesend Sea School and got trained there. Pretty tough it was too, like a borstal, so he says. They lived on an old training-ship. Terrible food and the instructors was bastards, give you a thumping soon as look at you. But it was all right once he got away at sea. The pay's not bad and if you're a steward there's a few chances for fiddling. I don't know about now though, with all them U-boats and torpedoes and things. I wouldn't fancy it myself."

"Do you know if they'll take people like me, with no experience and no training?"

Ray shrugged. "I don't know but I reckon they'd be glad to get anybody daft enough to do it these days. I tell you the place to find out. It's in London, down by the docks somewhere. I went there with Alec once when he'd landed at the East India docks. I think it's called the Shipping Federation. I'm not sure, but I think it's in Cable Street. Anyway, anybody'd tell you if you go to Aldgate East tube station and ask around there."

I felt excited, filled with a sense of limitless possibility. I had scarcely broken into the pound stolen from the Old Man's hoard. "Come on," I said, "let's have another. Have a whisky with it. I've got plenty of money."

By the time the pub closed I was slightly and pleasantly drunk. As Ray and I stood outside, waiting for our eyes to become accustomed to the dark and exchanging warm farewells and promises to meet again for a proper old piss-up, he said something which, for a few moments, tainted my euphoria with a tinge of sadness and regret. "Who's that nice lass I sometimes see you with, the one with the lovely pair of legs? If you want someone to look after her while you're away at sea I wouldn't mind doing

230

you a good turn." We both laughed but my laughter was simulated, and after Ray and I had parted and I was walking home I thought of Sally with pangs of jealous anger and longing and a dragging sense of loss.

Then, as I was turning into Kingsbury Square, I could just make out in the dark what looked like Kenneth's familiar shape and walk, and when I hurried to catch up I found that I had not been mistaken. He and his friend had been on a pub crawl so we were both a little inebriated as we went into the shop and climbed the stairs to the flat. The Old Man was sitting at the table smoking a cigarette and I knew as soon as I saw the expression on his face that he was in a bad mood.

He said, "Where have you two been till this time of night?"

"It's not very late," I said.

Kenneth did not say anything.

"You've been drinking again, haven't you?"

"I don't know what Kenneth's been doing. We just happened to get back at the same time." I answered. "I had a couple of halves with somebody from the boxing club."

"And who was that?"

"Ray Dixon."

"Ha! That street-corner boy! I might have guessed he's a boozer too. If you'd got any sense you'd steer clear of scum like that."

Kenneth was cutting himself a slice of bread obviously intent on not becoming involved. I was irritated by the Old Man's maligning of Ray. "He's a very nice bloke. I like him. And he's a good boxer too."

"Nice bloke! He's common as dirt." Then he turned his attention towards Kenneth. "And what've you been doing? I expect you've been swilling beer with a nice bloke too."

Kenneth was spreading meat paste on his slice of bread.

"I asked you a question!" the Old Man shouted.

"Oh, did you?" Kenneth said. "Sorry. What was it?" He took a bite and began to chew.

The Old Man's eyes bulged and he stood up. He looked for a moment as if he were about to attack his elder son, but he restrained himself and said through clenched teeth, "I asked you where you'd been. What you've been doing."

"I've been out with Geoff Copps. I thought you knew. He's on leave."

I took advantage of the Old Man's attention being focused on Kenneth and, murmuring that I was off to bed, I slipped out of the room.

I was climbing between the sheets when Kenneth came up.

I said, speaking quietly, "Looks as if she's shown him the door tonight, whoever she might be. What did he have to say about Geoff? Corner boy? Guttersnipe? Alcoholic?"

Kenneth grunted and began to undress. When he was in bed and the light was out I said, "Kenneth."

"What?" He sounded sleepy.

"Don't go to sleep. Listen. When he was out tonight I found where he keeps the tax-dodge money."

Kenneth did not reply for a few moments and I was

beginning to think that he had dozed off when he said, "Where? Where's he keep it? How much was it?"

We were whispering now. "In his wardrobe. I don't know how much. A lot. I reckon about four hundred quid."

"Christ!"

Neither of us spoke for a while. Then I whispered, "I think he owes us some, don't you?"

The answer I wanted to hear came after a couple of seconds: "Yes, I do."

I said, "We'll wait till Saturday. As soon as he's out of the way, in the dark-room or the studio, I'll grab some of it and we'll be off. We won't need to take anything with us. We'll be able to buy anything we need. We'll go to London, have a bit of a spree and then we'll join the Merchant Navy. How's that sound?"

"It sounds good," Kenneth said.

CHAPTER
TWELVE

The train rattled and swayed towards London through the grey and misty fields of Buckingham-shire. Kenneth and I had found a compartment to ourselves and we sat, facing each other, grinning with excitement.

"Come on," Kenneth said, "let's see it then."

From the inside breast pocket of my jacket I produced slowly, then with a conjuror's flourish, a wad of bank-notes.

"My God!" he said in a hushed voice. "How much is there? Did you take the lot?"

I shook my head. "No. I just grabbed some of it. Less than half. About a quarter, I should think."

"You might as well have taken the lot while you were at it."

"I couldn't. I don't know what stopped me."

"There's nothing he could do about it. He could hardly go to the police and say we'd pinched his tax-dodging money. They'd want to know where all that cash came from."

"We've got enough."

I could not explain why I had been unable to take the

full wallet because I did not myself quite understand what had prevented me. It was partly the sheer magnitude of the sum. The wallet had contained, at the lowest estimate, well over three hundred pounds and this was to me, at that time, a frighteningly large amount. In 1940 it would have been a pretty large sum to anyone, almost enough to buy a newly built small house, but this was not the only reason for my reluctance to take it all. Standing before the open wardrobe with dry mouth and hammering heartbeat I had felt, as I reached for the wallet, something like the same inhibition that had prevented me from hitting the Old Man with my full strength when we had fought on that summer night near Manor Road. Taking only a portion of the money was something like pulling my punch at the last moment had been.

"Come on," Kenneth said. "Let's count it."

I held the notes in my left hand and with my right I dealt them out, one for my brother and one for me, like playing cards or like, perhaps, the sweets we used to divide between us when we were much younger and could afford only one bag of lemon sherbets or liquorice torpedoes. When the spoils were divided each of us had thirty-seven pound-notes. We sat in silence for a few moments staring first at the money, then at each other with an amazement that was close to disbelief. And then we began to laugh and crow and leap up and down and prance around the compartment, thumping the padded seats until the swirling dust made us sneeze and we flopped down again, gasping and gleeful. When we had recovered from our dervish dance and were once more sitting grinning triumphantly at each other, Kenneth said, "I bet he's going to swing for us this time all right," and our laughter surged up again and, after it had subsided, it would erupt in little spurts every now and then for the rest of the journey to Baker Street Station.

It was the early afternoon when we arrived in London and walked all the way to Oxford Street, up to St Giles' Circus and along the Charing Cross Road towards Leicester Square. The streets were crowded with men and women in the uniform of the various armed services and with the usual civilian weekend shoppers and theatre-goers. The uniformed people carried their statutory respirators slung over one shoulder but not many civilians encumbered themselves with gas-masks in their cardboard boxes now that the early fears of poison-gas attacks had faded among all but the most pessimistic or irrationally frightened. In the sky above the roofs of shops and blocks of offices and flats the barrage balloons floated, becalmed, like plump dolphins, leaden-coloured and featureless. At the entrances to all the stores and offices were stacks of piled sandbags, and the plate-glass windows were patterned with adhesive tape to prevent splintering when the explosions occurred. But wartime drabness had not yet erased all colour and glamour from the surface of metropolitan life. Young women were still smartly dressed and there were some foreign uniforms among the khaki battledresses as well as the more brightly coloured indigenous uniforms of kilted Highlander and senior naval and army officers, braided and beribboned.

We had decided to stay at the Regent Palace Hotel in Piccadilly because I knew that we could easily afford to and, having spent a night with Sally at the almost identical Strand Palace, I felt that I would not be intimidated by the reception formalities. When we reached the hotel we went through the swing doors into the busy lobby, furnished and decorated with faded rococo elegance, and approached the reception desk where I asked the rather stern-looking woman in attendance for a double room with single beds.

"How long are you staying?" she asked.

"I'm not sure. At least three or four days."

I thought she was looking at us with suspicion. "Your luggage, sir?"

"At the station," I said. "We'll pick it up later."

She placed a key on the counter. "Room 107. The lift is over there on your right."

Kenneth and I went up to our room but stayed there only for a few moments.

I said, "We'd better do a bit of shopping. We need toothbrushes and shaving stuff. We'll get shirts and socks too. Then something to eat."

"And something to drink?" Kenneth suggested.

"We might do that as well," I said.

The weekend passed quickly. On the Sunday night there was a raid and we watched the gun-flashes in the sky and heard the explosions of the bombs falling in the East End, and I felt agreeably excited, almost as if we were witnessing a dramatic simulacrum, a play or movie, rather than a holocaust in which people were really suffering and dying. It was perhaps the distance between us in the West End and the place where the bombs were falling and the fact that neither Kenneth nor I had ever seen, at close quarters, what those high explosives could do to people and to their homes that neutralized the imagination and stifled all but a superficial sympathy. Or maybe it was simply the callow selfishness of youth, for, when we saw at night the platforms of the underground stations filled with people, young children and old men and women who might have been their grandparents, lying in irregular packed rows beneath blankets in their improvised beds, I felt little more than the curiosity of a tourist visiting the catacombs.

During the next few days Kenneth and I seemed to let ourselves drift on a mildly sybaritic tide of self-indulgence and we found that even in wartime London there was much to tempt us. First the bookshops in Charing Cross Road drew us irresistibly and for many hours into their dim and well-stocked interiors. I now remember only a few of the titles of the books we bought: *Palgrave's Golden Treasury*, Yeats's *Oxford Book of Modern Verse*, and some Penguin novels including Eric Linklater's *Poet's Pub*, Aldous Huxley's *Crome Yellow* and Stella Gibbons's *Cold Comfort Farm*. What now seems almost inexplicable was another choice of ours, a novel called *The Hill is Mine* by the then very popular writer, long since forgotten, Maurice Walsh,

238

whose books we had enjoyed when younger. I came across one of this author's novels in a second-hand bookshop a few years after the war and a glance at the first few pages left me mystified as to the attraction he once held for Kenneth and me, and I could only think that we had, at that stage, much less discernment than we believed we possessed. His style, which, as far as I recall, was a weirdly artificial mish-mash of parodied J. M. Synge and Marie Corelli, was used in the service of intensely romantic tales set in the wilder regions of a never-never Ireland.

Another odd purchase we made at this time was an ex-army kitbag. I can quite see why we needed a receptacle of some kind in which to carry our accumulating possessions but why we did not buy something more easily carried, a grip or a rucksack, I cannot now understand. It is possible, I suppose, that, finding we were spending our money quite rapidly, we decided to economize and buy the cheapest form of luggage available, and certainly the kitbag was inexpensive. Later we were to regret the economy, if that is what it was.

The bookshops were not the only places of entertainment that beguiled us. We went to various cinemas and saw more movies in those few days than we had seen in the past couple of months and, less frivolously, we saw Donald Wolfit's celebrated — some might say notorious —*King Lear*, and we went to the National Gallery to hear some of Myra Hess's lunchtime recitals. In the evenings we embarked on pub crawls in Soho and every night we ended up in the garish glitter of the Piccadilly Lyons

Corner House and ate meals that would have horrified a dietician as much as they delighted us. Then, on Friday morning, we woke with mild hangovers and the shared feeling that it was about time we did something constructive about our future.

We counted our money and found that, while we were still relatively well-off, we had spent an alarmingly large amount in a very short time, and we had to remember that we still had the hotel bill to pay. We had allowed ourselves to be seduced by the temptations afforded by our temporary affluence but must now apply ourselves to the serious business of joining the Merchant Navy. So we took the underground train to Aldgate East and set off in search of the Shipping Federation offices, which we found without too much difficulty. On our journey in search of them we saw plenty of evidence of German bombing in cordoned-off ruined buildings, areas of wasteland where, until recently, shops, factories and warehouses had stood, and side streets where many of the little houses in the terraces had been smashed down to their knees like gap-toothed supplicants.

Our interview with the uniformed officer at the Federation was brief and humiliating. When I told him that we wanted to go to sea he looked at us with faintly amused surprise and an almost imperceptible slow shaking of the head and said, "As what?"

I looked at Kenneth for help but he had none to offer.

"Well," I said, "anything really, I mean, there must be jobs for unskilled people. Deckhands. In the galley . . . er . . . anything."

Suddenly he looked less amiable. "Deckhands aren't unskilled," he said carefully. "There isn't anybody in a ship's company that's unskilled. What use do you think you'd be at sea? You don't look used to hard work, either of you. Take my advice and go home and wait till you're called up. You're wasting your time and mine here."

Back in the street we walked a few paces in embarrassed silence.

Then I said, "Smug bastard. He didn't look such a tough old sea-dog. I bet it's a long time since he was on a ship and even then I expect he was a purser or something. Sod him."

"I think we need a drink. They'll be open now," said Kenneth.

I nodded and, as I began to look around for a pub sign, I heard behind us quick footsteps drawing close and then a man's voice calling, "Hey! You two! Just a minute!"

Kenneth and I stopped and looked round at the man approaching us. He seemed to be in his late thirties and was wearing old and unmatching suit-trousers and jacket and a dark blue woollen sweater. His face was lean and unshaven and his smile, which was probably meant to be ingratiating, showed broken and decaying teeth and was too much like a snarl to be reassuring. But his manner was friendly enough when he joined us where we were standing and began to speak.

"I saw you two lads in there. Couldn't help hearing what you was saying to that bloke about getting a ship. You'll never get one that way, not with them lot. Too much red tape. You've got to have a seaman's book and all that stuff. But if you really want to get a ship there's ways of doing it. Nothing easier, if you know how."

"How do you get one then?" Kenneth asked, and I thought I heard a note of scepticism in his voice.

"Dead easy. Listen. We can't talk here like this, can we? Let's go and have a chat somewhere quiet. There's a nice little pub not far from here. I'm a regular. When I'm ashore, that is. OK?"

I said, "All right. We were going for a drink anyway."

"My name's Bill," our guide told us, "Bill Whitely. I been at sea for nigh on twenty years so I know the ropes, as you might say."

When we reached the pub and were standing at the bar Bill surprised me by asking, "What will you have then, lads?" I had assumed that we would be expected to pay and indeed had suspected that his sole reason for asking us to accompany him had been to solicit a free drink.

We were all served with pints of bitter which we carried to a table, where we sat down.

"Cheers!" he said and gave us his terrible, decayed smile. I was beginning to warm to him a little, feeling rather as one feels towards a very unprepossessing dog who is anxious for affection.

I said, "Are you ashore for long?"

"A couple of weeks. Then I sail for Aden on a tanker. But listen. You and your mate — or are you brothers?" I nodded. "Yeah, thought you was. You both want to get to sea, don't you? Don't blame you neither. It's a great life, even now, in wartime. But you'll never get away from here, not from London. Place you want to go to's Cardiff. You'll get a ship there if you know how to set about it. And that's where I can help you."

I took a drink of my beer. "How?"

"No red tape. There's always ships left short-handed the day they're sailing. Skipper always glad to get anybody. You won't need papers nor nothing. But you do need to know where to go. Right?"

We waited for more information.

"There's an old shipmate of mine, a good bit older than me. He's settled down ashore, got himself a caff in Bute Street. That's near the docks in Cardiff. What they call Tiger Bay. He'll fix you up. Portuguese Joe's what they call him. Anybody'll tell you where the caff is. You go down Bute Street and ask anybody where Portuguese Joe's is. They'll tell you. He's fixed up lots of young blokes that want to get away to sea. I sent someone down to Joe's place last time I was ashore and I know for a fact he fixed him up."

"But we've got no experience," I said.

"Don't worry. You're both big strong lads. Don't take no notice what that silly sod told you back there. Any skipper looking for crew wouldn't think twice. He'd be lucky to get you."

We finished our beers and I bought a second round. When I was back in my seat Bill said, "All the best, shipmates!" and took a long pull at his pint. Then he went on: "No, you don't have to worry about experience. Long as you're willing. Mind you, never try and bluff an old seaman. Some of 'em try it on, you know. Only the other night I was in here and got talking to a bloke reckoned he'd just come back from Australia. Told me he was a trimmer."

"What's a trimmer?" I asked.

"He's the bloke that feeds the coal to the stoker. He's got to keep the supply steady, keep it trimmed. That's why he's called the trimmer. Anyway he reckons he was on the *Duke of Cornwall*. I says to him, 'What? You was on the *Cornwall* as a trimmer?' 'That's right,' he says. 'You're a fucking liar,' I says. 'The *Cornwall*'s a bleeding oil-burner.' See? You don't get no coal on an oil-burner. He couldn't have been a fucking trimmer 'cos there wouldn't be no coal to trim!"

I said, "If we go and see your friend, Joe, what do we say exactly?"

"Just tell him I sent you. Say Bill Whitely sent you. Tell him you want to get a ship. You don't mind where she's bound for or what you sail as. He'll see you're all right." He took another swig, almost emptying his glass. "Of course, Joe's going to expect you to slip him a few quid. You don't get anything for nothing in this world."

"Oh," I said. Then: "How much?"

"A fiver should do it."

"For each of us, or for both?"

"Listen, you tell him you're friends of mine and I don't suppose he'll ask for more than a fiver for the pair of you." His face split into that charnel smile again. "Hey, drink up, lads. Let's have another."

We drained our glasses and Bill stood, reached out and picked them up with his own and turned towards the bar. He took two paces and then stopped abruptly, came back to the table, and replaced the glasses.

"Christ!" he said. "I've just remembered, lads. I've only got a few coppers left. Don't get me wrong. I've got plenty at home but I just forgot to bring it. Well, I didn't really forget. I just didn't bring it. I never expected to meet anybody this morning. I was going to go straight back home after I'd checked at the Shipping Federation, see if there was any message for me. Sorry, we'll have to skip this one. Maybe we can —" He broke off in mid-sentence and his expression suddenly became one of wondering conjecture: "Hey! I don't suppose you lads could lend me a few bob? Pity to break up this little party. I tell you what. I'll see you tonight, here or up West if you like. Pay you back. How'd that be?"

Kenneth and I exchanged questioning and embarrassed looks.

Bill sensed the uncertainty and pressed on: "It'd only be for a few hours. Just to see us through the morning like."

I said, "How much do you want?"

"A couple of quid'd be fine."

He could see that I was reflecting that two pounds was more than enough for a whole week's supply of beer and he said quickly, "That'll see us through this morning and I'll be able to do a bit of shopping for my old mum. She can't get about these days, poor old dear. Don't worry about me paying you back, son. I've got plenty at home. We can meet in here tonight or, like I said, up West. I wouldn't mind a night on the town, come to think of it. Tell you what. I'll see you tonight in the Intrepid Fox. That's not far from the Windmill. Anybody'll tell you where it is. OK?"

I averted my eyes from his smile and produced two pound-notes and handed them over. He went to the bar and came back with our drinks and a packet of cigarettes which he opened and generously handed round. He stayed with us for another round, bought by Kenneth, and then left with cheery assurances that we would meet at seven-thirty in the evening and have a really good night out.

When he had gone Kenneth said, "Do you think we'll ever see him again?"

"I doubt it," I answered, after a moment's thought. And of course we never did.

It was towards the end of the following week that we realized that our money was running short and we would have to get out of the hotel and make another and more determined attempt at going to sea. We wondered if Bill's story of Portuguese Joe's café in Cardiff had contained any truth at all and finally decided, though not very confidently, that it might not have been pure invention and it was worth a try. So we left London for Cardiff, taking it in turns to carry our kitbag, which was by now quite heavy with the books and extra clothes we had acquired.

In Cardiff we took a room in a cheap bed-and-breakfast place, and on the night of our arrival, we set out to find Portuguese Joe's. It was by now December and the darkness of the black-out was augmented by heavy mist from the sea to make our search more difficult. Finding

Bute Street was easy, but the locating of Portuguese Joe's, if such a place existed, presented more serious problems. We made our stumbling way along the greasy pavements and, on the few occasions when footsteps of other wayfarers were heard, we called out for information about Portuguese Joe's café, each time becoming more conscious of the comic-strip absurdity of the name. "Might as well be asking for Buffalo Bill's," Kenneth commented morosely.

We were ready to abandon the search when we found, directed to it by the sound of male voices raised in song, a public house which we gratefully entered. The bar was noisy and crowded but warm and welcoming. We bought a couple of pints of bitter and felt our despondency gradually lifting under alcohol's beneficent influence. After a second pint I felt relaxed enough to chat with another drinker at the bar, an amiable-looking man in what I guessed was his late forties, whose tough, weathered features might be those of a seafaring man. We exchanged remarks about the weather and I admitted, on being asked if this was so, that I was English.

Then I said, "I don't suppose you happen to know of a café around here called Portuguese Joe's?"

He looked at me sharply. "Portuguese Joe's? Yes, I know it. Turn right when you get out of here. It's about fifty yards along the same side. What d'you want to know for?"

I said to Kenneth, "You hear that? He knows Portuguese Joe's!"

The man repeated, "Why you asking about it?"

I hesitated before answering. Then I said, "Somebody

247

we met in London — a sailor — told us. He said we might be able to get a ship if we went there and saw this bloke Joe."

"You been to sea?"

"No."

"Then you won't get a ship, not from Cardiff."

"The man I met said Portuguese Joe could fix it for us."

"Did he?" The man smiled faintly. "I'd keep away from there if I was you, boyo. It's not a very nice place, not nice at all." Then he added, "I've heard of ships taking on hands at Glasgow or Greenock without sea books. I couldn't swear it's true, though."

Kenneth and I finished our drinks, said goodnight, and left the pub.

Outside I said, "What do you think?"

"We've come all this way. We might as well go and see what happens. Give it a try."

"OK."

We made our way along the street, peering through the darkness and the mist which seemed to cling to the face like clammy webs, and after a few minutes we came to the café, pushed open the door and went inside where we stood for a moment blinking in the smoke-curdled light. There were eight tables with imitation marble tops, stained and dirty, four on each side of the room, and at the end farthest from the door was a counter with an ancient cash-register on one end and a closed serving-hatch behind it. Every table was occupied by men of almost uniformly sinister aspect, though no one was eating. Some of the customers had thick cups of dark liquid, perhaps tea or coffee, in front of them; others were playing cards. Everyone was smoking. As we closed the door behind us all heads either raised or turned and we found ourselves the focal point of a fixed and unfriendly scrutiny. Behind the counter, leaning on the elbows of his folded arms, was the man we took to be the proprietor, Portuguese Joe himself. He was partly bald, swarthy and stockily built. The forearms on the counter looked massive. No one spoke.

Kenneth and I advanced towards him. He did not move but stared at us steadily as we approached.

I waited, hoping Kenneth would speak but he remained silent, like everyone else.

I said, "Excuse me . . ." and as soon as I had spoken I knew that the deferential approach was not the one I should have chosen, ". . . are you Portuguese Joe?"

I sounded ridiculous, even to myself.

The man still said nothing and continued to stare at us with his hard, black little eyes, expressionless except for a hint of contempt and latent hostility.

I gabbled on: "Bill Whitely in London — says he's an old friend of yours — we met him at the Shipping Federation. Looking for a ship. I mean we were. Looking for a ship. He said you could help, maybe. We know we'd have to give you something. Pay, I mean. He said about a fiver. Is that all right? W'd be very grateful. If you could help . . . do you . . . I mean is there . . . any chance of . . ." My voice tottered to an uneasy halt.

Portuguese Joe went on staring at us. So did everyone else in the café. And still no one said a word.

Then a voice did speak. It was Kenneth's. He muttered,

"Come on. Let's go!" and we both turned away from the counter and walked quickly to the door along the narrow aisle between the tables of silent, staring customers.

Outside in the cold darkness I released the breath which I had not realized I had been holding in a long exhalation of relief.

Kenneth said, "I don't think they liked us very much in there," and, as we walked away, we heard from inside the café a rumbling noise of voices rising in what was unmistakably a chorus of derisory laughter.

On our way back to where we were staying, near the central railway station, we stopped at a pub for a consolatory couple of drinks over which we discussed what next we should do. I remembered that the man in the bar in Bute Street, who had directed us to Portuguese Joe's, had said that he had heard of people being taken on by captains of ships at Glasgow docks. Perhaps we should try our luck there.

Kenneth agreed, though he did not sound optimistic.

The pub we were now drinking in was quite large and there seemed to be a lot of high-spirited laughter and general conviviality, which tended to darken our gloom. And then I noticed, sitting at a table not far from us, with a couple of soldiers, two girls one of whom looked for a moment of heart-jolting recognition almost exactly like Sally. A second glance modified that first impression but some similarity remained: she had the same slightly up-tilted little nose and the small yet ripe mouth, and something of Sally's oddly provocative impassivity.

That night I found it difficult to sleep. I had often

thought of Sally since our flight from Aylesbury but the excitement and variety of my new affluent life in London had largely protected me against deep feelings of longing or loss. But now that money was running low and prospects were grimly uncertain I was suddenly more vulnerable to these emotions and I lay miserably listening to the moaning of fog-horns from the Bristol Channel and visualizing Sally in her bed, sleeping peacefully, untouched by regret for my departure or concern for my wellbeing or — far more painful to contemplate — lying with someone, Ronald Kirk perhaps, her lovely, round, plump little buttocks tucked snugly into his groin as she nestled in his arms. For the first time since Kenneth and I had boarded the train for Baker Street at Aylesbury Station I had doubts as to the wisdom of our robbing the Old Man and leaving Kingsbury Square, and only when at last I fell asleep was I rescued from the toils of self-pity, sexual longing, jealousy and uncertainty as to what the future held.

The next day, however, I felt reasonably cheerful and Kenneth and I were able to joke about our pathetic performance in Portuguese Joe's café. So we set off, lugging in turns our kitbag, for Glasgow, arriving in the early evening and, after tramping the streets for an hour or so, we were able to find a room in an old Victorian boarding-house. The weather here was much colder than in Wales and the next day, when we found our way to the docks, I realized that the sole of one of my shoes was admitting moisture from the pavements. Our attempts to be taken on as seamen were no more than perfunctory and I am sure that we both knew, even before our efforts were rebuffed, that a life at sea was not going to materialize.

The weather grew worse as Christmas approached and we decided that we could not afford new footwear for me so I had to make do with a piece of cardboard inside my right shoe, which provided little or no protection when, as occurred almost daily, the rain came down. Despite the cold and wet we both liked Glasgow. What impressed and surprised me was the sense of foreignness that I felt almost the moment I left the train. This was not caused simply by the strange accent and speech-patterns we heard all around us, nor by the dietary peculiarities — the salty porridge, the "mealy puddens", mutton pies and baps; nor was it caused by the prevalence of Tam o' Shanters or "Balmorals", those pancake-shaped bonnets with a pompon in the centre worn by infantrymen in Scottish regiments — unless they were sporting the more colourful "dress" glengarry, the cap like a small inverted boat with ribbons hanging down behind; though all of these things, I suppose, contributed to my feeling of being in another country, a sensation quite different from anything I had experienced in Wales. Quite apart from their speech, the people seemed different from the English, though I could not precisely define their difference, which seemed to be connected perhaps with traditions of forthrightness, hospitality and a highly developed sense of national identity. Whatever its cause the feeling was pleasantly stimulating and I was never wholly to lose it.

Kenneth and I found that our days in Glasgow began

to take on a repetitive shape. We had originally started to use the public library in order to avail ourselves of the daily newspapers in the reading-room, hoping we might find work advertised in the Situations Vacant columns, but, after the first three or four mornings, when we came across no job that either of us felt he could apply for, we gave up even a pretence of continuing the search. We still went to the library each day after breakfast but now we sat and read first the daily news and then settled down to enjoy whatever books we had selected from the shelves devoted to English literature. On the relatively rare afternoons when it was not raining or sleeting we walked the streets without definite purpose, yet vaguely hopeful that some lucky encounter might provide a way of escape from the bleak, immitigable predicament that our folly and ineptitude had created.

It was only a few days before Christmas, when our last week in the room for which we had prepaid the rent was about to expire and we found that we possessed between us scarcely enough cash to buy us both a meal, that a way, not so much of escape as of solving immediate problems, presented itself. We were, through habit, walking towards the library when we noticed something that we must have seen a dozen times before without consciously registering its existence: it was an army recruiting office. This time we stopped and looked into the window behind which various posters were displayed. One of these was headed with the words: "Are you Over 18 and Under 20? If you are you can join a Young Soldiers' Battalion". More details followed in smaller print.

We looked at each other.

"What about that?" I said. "At least I'd get some shoes without holes."

"Boots," Kenneth corrected me. Then: "I'm over twenty."

I had picked up from somewhere the information — incidentally, fallacious — that twins in the army could not be separated. I said, "Why don't we say we're the same age? People think we look alike. I don't think they'd question it."

We hesitated. The army was the one service I had sworn that I would never join, but, I told myself, a Scottish regiment would be different, more glamorous. And my feet would be dry and warm.

"Come on," I urged.

The recruiting officer did not show the least disbelief when we gave the same date of birth. We were medically examined and passed as A1. We signed the appropriate forms and were given a travel warrant to Stonehaven, where we were to report to the 70th Battalion Argyll and Sutherland Highlanders, stationed at the Bay Hotel. Our train left Glasgow Central Station at three-fifteen.

Back in the street, I said, "Bay Hotel, eh? That should be nice and comfortable," and I meant what I said, ignorant and deluded youth that I was.

We went back to our room to collect our belongings and wait until it was time to begin our next journey, which would take us to places not inscribed on any travel warrant, and would prove to be much longer and stranger than either of us could have ever guessed.

LARGE PRINT

ISIS publish a wide range of books in large print, from fiction to biography. A full list of titles is available free of charge from the address below. Alternatively, contact your local library for details of their collection of ISIS books.

Details of ISIS unabridged audio books are also available.

Any suggestions for books you would like to see in large print or audio are always welcome.

ISIS
7 Centremead
Osney Mead
Oxford OX2 0ES
(0865) 250333

BIOGRAPHY AND AUTOBIOGRAPHY

BIOGRAPHY AND AUTOBIOGRAPHY

Paul James	**Margaret**
Paul James	**Princess Alexandra**
John Kerr	**Queen Victoria's Scottish Diaries**
Margaret Lane	**The Tale of Beatrix Potter**
Bernard Levin	**The Way We Live Now**
Margaret Lewis	**Ngaio Marsh**
Vera Lynn	**Unsung Heroines**
Peter Medawar	**Memoir of a Thinking Radish**
Michael Nicholson	**Natasha's Story**
Angela Patmore	**Marje**
Marjorie Quarton	**Saturday's Child**
Martyn Shallcross	**The Private World of Daphne Du Maurier**
Frank and Joan Shaw	**We Remember the Blitz**
Joyce Storey	**Our Joyce**
Douglas Sutherland	**Born Yesterday**
James Whitaker	**Diana v. Charles**

(A) Large Print books also available in Audio

BIOGRAPHY AND AUTOBIOGRAPHY

David Bret	**Maurice Chevalier**
Sven Broman	**Garbo on Garbo**
Pauline Collins	**Letter to Louise**
Earl Conrad	**Errol Flynn**
Quentin Falk	**Anthony Hopkins**
Clive Fisher	**Noël Coward**
Sir John Gielgud	**Backward Glances**
Reggie Grenfell & Richard Garnett	
	Joyce By Herself and Her Friends (A)
Michael Hordern	**A World Elsewhere**
Joanna Lumley	**Stare Back and Smile**
Shirley MacLaine	**Dance While You Can**
Arthur Marshall	**Follow the Sun**
Sheriday Morley	**Robert, My Father**
Michael Munn	**Hollywood Rogues**
Peter O'Toole	**Loitering With Intent**
Adua Pavarotti	**Pavarotti**
Hilton Tims	**Once a Wicked Lady**
Peter Underwood	**Death in Hollywood**
Alexander Walker	**Elizabeth**
Aissa Wayne	**John Wayne, My Father**
Jane Ellen Wayne	**Clark Gable**
Jane Ellen Wayne	**The Life and Loves of Grace Kelly**

WORLD WAR II

Paul Brickhill	**The Dam Busters**
Reinhold Eggers	**Escape From Colditz**
Fey von Hassell	**A Mother's War**
Dorothy Brewer Kerr	**The Girls Behind the Guns**
Vera Lynn	**We'll Meet Again** (A)
Vera Lynn	**Unsung Heroines**
Tom Quinn	**Sea War**
Frank and Joan Shaw	**We Remember the Battle of Britain**
Frank and Joan Shaw	**We Remember the Blitz**
Frank and Joan Shaw	**We Remember D-Day**
William Sparks	**The Last of the Cockleshell Heroes**
Anne Valery	**Talking About the War**

POETRY

**Long Remembered:
Narrative Poems**

INSPIRATIONAL

Thora Hird	**Thora Hird's Praise Be! Notebook**

REFERENCE AND DICTIONARIES

The Longman English Dictionary
The Longman Medical Dictionary

TRAVEL, ADVENTURE AND EXPLORATION

Jacques Cousteau	**The Silent World**
Peter Davies	**The Farms of Home**
Patrick Leigh Fermor	**Three Letters From the Andes**
Keath Fraser	**Worst Journeys**
John Hillaby	**Journey to the Gods**
Dervla Murphy	**The Ukimwi Road**
Freya Stark	**The Southern Gates of Arabia**
Tom Vernon	**Fat Man in Argentina**
A Wainwright	**Wainwright in the Limestone Dales**
Dylan Winter	**A Hack in the Borders**

(A) Large Print books also available in Audio

HEALTH AND SELF HELP

Dr Anthony Campbell	**Getting the Best For Your Bad Back**
Dr Joan Gomez	*Sixty*something
Wendy and Sally Greengross	**Living, Loving and Ageing**
Margaret Hills	**Curing Arthritis**
	Longman Medical Dictionary
Dr Geoffrey Littlejohn	**Rheumatism**
Kenneth Lysons	**Earning Money in Retirement**
Dr Brice Pitt	**Making the Most of Middle Age**
Neville Shone	**Coping Successfully With Pain**
Dr Tom Smith	**Heart Attacks**
Nancy Tuft	**Looking Good, Feeling Good**
Denys Wainwright	**Arthritis and Rheumatism**
Claire Weekes	**More Help for Your Nerves**

GENERAL NON-FICTION

Eric Delderfield	**Eric Delderfield's Bumper Book of True Animal Stories**
Caroline Elliot	**The BBC Book of Royal Memories 1947-1990**
Joan Grant	**The Cuckoo on the Kettle**
Joan Grant	**The Owl on the Teapot**
Helene Hanff	**Letters From New York**
Martin Lloyd-Elliott	**City Ablaze**
Elizabeth Longford	**Royal Throne**
Joanna Lumley	**Forces Sweethearts**
Vera Lynn	**We'll Meet Again**
Desmond Morris	**The Animal Contract**
Anne Scott-James and Osbert Lancaster	
	The Pleasure Garden
Les Stocker	**The Hedgehog and Friends**
Elisabeth Svendsen	**Down Among the Donkeys**
Gloria Wood and Paul Thompson	**The Nineties**
The Lady Wardington	**Superhints for Gardeners**
Nicholas Witchell	**The Loch Ness Story**